"The Object Lessons series achieves something very close to magic: the books take ordinary—even banal—objects and animate them with a rich history of invention, political struggle, science, and popular mythology. Filled with fascinating details and conveyed in sharp, accessible prose, the books make the everyday world come to life. Be warned: once you've read a few of these, you'll start walking around your house, picking up random objects, and musing aloud: 'I wonder what the story is behind this thing?'"

Steven Johnson, author of *Where Good Ideas Come From* and *How We Got to Now*

"In 1957 the French critic and semiotician Roland Barthes published *Mythologies*, a groundbreaking series of essays in which he analysed the popular culture of his day, from laundry detergent to the face of Greta Garbo, professional wrestling to the Citroën DS. This series of short books, Object Lessons, continues the tradition."

Melissa Harrison, *Financial Times*

"Though short, at roughly 25,000 words apiece, these books are anything but slight."

Marina Benjamin, *New Statesman*

"The joy of the series, of reading *Remote Control, Golf Ball, Driver's License, Drone, Silence, Glass, Refrigerator, Hotel*, and *Waste* (more titles are listed as forthcoming) in quick succession, lies in encountering the various turns through which each of their authors has been put by his or her object. As for Benjamin, so for the authors of the series, the object predominates, sits squarely center stage, directs the action. The object decides the genre, the chronology, and the limits of the study. Accordingly, the author has to take her cue from the *thing* she chose or that chose her. The result is a wonderfully uneven series of books, each one a *thing* unto itself."

Julian Yates, *Los Angeles Review of Books*

"The Object Lessons project, edited by game theory legend Ian Bogost and cultural studies academic Christopher Schaberg, commissions short essays and small, beautiful books about everyday objects from shipping containers to toast. *The Atlantic* hosts a collection of "mini object-lessons"... More substantive is Bloomsbury's collection of small, gorgeously designed books that delve into their subjects in much more depth."

Cory Doctorow, *Boing Boing*

OBJECTLESSONS

A book series about the hidden lives of ordinary things.

Series Editors:

Ian Bogost and Christopher Schaberg

Advisory Board:

Sara Ahmed, Jane Bennett, Jeffrey Jerome Cohen,
Johanna Drucker, Raiford Guins, Graham Harman,
renée hoogland, Pam Houston, Eileen Joy, Douglas
Kahn, Daniel Miller, Esther Milne, Timothy Morton,
Kathleen Stewart, Nigel Thrift, Rob Walker, Michele White.

In association with

Georgia Tech | Center for Media Studies

BOOKS IN THE SERIES

password

MARTIN PAUL EVE

Bloomsbury Academic

An imprint of Bloomsbury Publishing Inc

B L O O M S B U R Y

NEW YORK · LONDON · OXFORD · NEW DELHI · SYDNEY

Bloomsbury Academic

An imprint of Bloomsbury Publishing Inc

1385 Broadway	50 Bedford Square
New York	London
NY 10018	WC1B 3DP
USA	UK

www.bloomsbury.com

First published 2016

Library of Congress Cataloging-in-Publication Data
Names: Eve, Martin Paul, 1986- author.
Title: Password / Martin Paul Eve.
Description: New York, NY, USA : Bloomsbury Academic, 2016. | Series: Object
lessons : a book series about the hidden lives of ordinary things | Includes
bibliographical references and index.
Identifiers: LCCN 2015046301 (print) | LCCN 2015048632 (ebook) |
ISBN 9781501314872 (pbk. : alk. paper) | ISBN 9781501314889 (ePub) |
ISBN 9781501314896 (ePDF)
Subjects: LCSH: Identification–Popular works. | Passing (Identity)–Popular
works. | Authentication–Popular works. | Security systems–Popular works. |
Computers–Access control–Passwords–Popular works.
Classification: LCC HM1068 .E93 2016 (print) | LCC HM1068 (ebook) |
DDC 005.8–dc23
LC record available at http://lccn.loc.gov/2015046301

ISBN: PB: 978-1-5013-1487-2
ePub: 978-1-5013-1488-9
ePDF: 978-1-5013-1489-6

Series: Object Lessons

Cover design: Alice Marwick
Cover image © Alice Marwick

Typeset by Deanta Global Publishing Services, Chennai, India
Printed and bound in the United States of America

For Helen

echo "U2FsdGVkX1/HPZfS0ZjSQAVikQ7iyPB79Vy
M3FoZASc+bw92R8K4izi6ayLe/OOp" |

openssl enc -d -aes-256-cbc -a -salt

All author royalties from this book will be donated
to Arthritis Research UK.

CONTENTS

INTRODUCTION: PASSWORDS AND THEIR LIMITS

FIGURE 1 Laberinto 1 (del Nordisk familjebok) by Sebastián Asegurado. Image out of copyright (public domain).

In Ancient Crete, mythology tells us, Theseus journeyed deep into a labyrinth in order to slay a ferocious half-man, half-bull beast called the Minotaur – a bit unfair on the Minotaur perhaps, but fourteen young men and women were sacrificed to feed it as retribution for the death of Minos's son Androgeos. Yet the labyrinth was said to be so impenetrable that even its creator, Daedalus, was scarcely able to escape after its construction; Daedalus was saved only by his foreknowledge of the maze. In the myth, Theseus knew the danger of this spatial arrangement for his plan and with the help of a ball of thread charted his own progress through the labyrinth so that he might re-trace his steps, once the task was complete.

The labyrinth is a brilliant plot device for a myth because it gives a clear driver for dramatic action. The very existence of a labyrinth poses an irresistible navigational challenge that provides motive for character action within a story. Indeed, the basic rules of literary economy dictate that if a labyrinth is present, a hero must solve it. In this way, the labyrinth is the type of plot device that almost makes the hero; the subject-position 'questing hero' is created by the challenge of and response to the maze. The labyrinth is also useful for writers because it allows for the unambiguous sorting of individuals who respond to this challenge: those who can navigate the maze and those who cannot. Typically the hero must end up in the former category while there will be many indirect narrations of those who have failed in order to further legitimate the success and uniqueness of the protagonist.

For playful twentieth-century writers like Jorge Luis Borges, Alain Robbe-Grillet, or even Kate Mosse – all of whom have works that feature the word 'labyrinth' in their titles – the labyrinth might be posed as the ultimate mirror of literature itself.

Yet Daedalus's labyrinth was nominally supposed to serve a single purpose within the tale: to ensure that one being – and only one being (Daedalus) – could ever get out. In this way it would contain the Minotaur and the sacrificial victims. The labyrinth was designed as a spatial-control mechanism for determining the unique identity of a single individual based on knowledge of its topology. In this regard, it had to be (and was) a failure so that Theseus could emerge as the hero. For everyone but Daedalus, the labyrinth was supposed to be, quite literally, a death trap. In the story, Theseus found a way to circumvent the labyrinth's identification function through a cunning appreciation of the fact that the maze was in one sense symmetrical; the same route that lets you in can get you out. In this way the hero responds correctly to the challenge of the impossible maze: the flaws of a labyrinth as a means to identify individuals with cartographic knowledge are laid bare.

While the Theseus myth has stood the test of time and does much for Crete's tourist industry, the labyrinth also looks a lot like something else with which we are all acquainted. In its planned function of identification through the proxy of knowledge and its implicit offer of a topological challenge to which a successful navigation constitutes a correct response, the labyrinth resembles the special type of control system that we call a password. Theseus, on the other hand, is one of the earliest species of geek that we now would call a hacker or cracker.

•••• _

Now consider a second story. A citizen of the United Kingdom sits alone at his computer, early in the twenty-first century (but most likely late at night). His name is Gary McKinnon and he is obsessed by the idea that the US government is covering up evidence of extraterrestrial life. Before him on his screen is a password prompt for an American military computer that he is remotely accessing: the familiar blinking cursor. '•••• _'. In this case, McKinnon does not type a password but simply hits [ENTER] because he knows the password is blank. In fact, he has spent weeks running a basic script of his own devising to trawl through known addresses of US military systems. This script was automatically looking for the instances where the careless security practice of empty passwords had left the lock wide open (surely an instance of what Tung-Hui Hu has charted within an alarming discourse of bad 'digital hygiene').[1]

Like Theseus, McKinnon perceived of himself as a hero of sorts. In McKinnon's case, it was a belief in a quest for truth against the Minotaur of the US government. The challenge that legitimated his quest and that hailed him as a questing hero-subject was the message 'PASSWORD', the irresistible lure to demonstrate knowledge to prove one's worthiness and thereby gain access. Similarly, his Theseus-like moment of cunning was to find a way around the maze that did not involve knowing the pre-shared secret in advance. Indeed, McKinnon's technique was simply to push at all the doors in the (correctly placed) hope that someone had negligently left some wide open.

Two different contexts, separated by a vast time period, but united in a common narrative: in the challenge/response formulation, various platforms that desire to identify individuals based on their knowledge also cry out to be defeated. Compared to McKinnon's hacking, the labyrinth, then, is one of the best examples of the fact that different cultures in different epochs have invariably needed to identify friend from foe, and that this need has usually been met through a restriction of knowledge. Indeed, mechanisms that function in the same way as 'passwords' have existed across time and space, from Ancient Rome and Greece through to the contemporary systems of authentication with which we are all by now thoroughly familiar. As the labyrinth demonstrates, passwords have also never taken a single form (pass-'word' is actually a misnomer) and this looks set to continue to mutate in the future: 'Your password is your face,' scream Microsoft billboards aside London buses. Yet we rarely consider passwords – devices that distinguish between individuals based on knowledge – as anything but the obvious and natural way in which we might identify someone, the clear solution to the problem. Consider only that it is now so ingrained to think of passwords as verifying somebody's identity that we can say without batting an eyelid that if someone's password is compromised their identity has been 'stolen'.

But passwords are far from obvious, natural or simple. Passwords are complex social assemblages shaped by and shaping religious histories, myth, literatures of magic and fantasy, bodies, subjects and personhood. They offer us glimpses into a fundamental problem for our increasingly quantified age: Just what does it mean to talk about someone's 'identity'?

••••_

If you needed to verify someone's claim to be a specific individual, how would *you* go about it?

Many methods spring to mind. If you know the person and are face-to-face, you might rely on sight, provided you can see. If you cannot see, you might ask him or her to speak, recognizing by voice, provided you can hear. Powerful and wealthy entities such as governments use sophisticated identity cards, linked to family records uniquely available to the state, with supposedly tamper-proof photographic or biometric data. However, assuming that you lacked such power and wealth, or that you were at great distance from the person in question, or even that you did not intimately know the individual in advance, it is likely that you would arrange a system of identification based on a challenge to communicate pre-shared knowledge: a password.

Using a password usually consists of two components: issuing a challenge and receiving a response. The person wishing to confirm the identity of another will ask for the password. The respondent is then supposed to give the agreed pre-shared knowledge to demonstrate his or her identity. Fundamentally, a correct response to a password challenge verifies that an individual *knows* a specific word or phrase. If it is believed that one and only one individual could know the password, then it is assumed that this knowledge identifies that person. If the password is known more broadly, however, then this is likely to result in a misidentification.

Passwords seem to be uncontentious. They are ubiquitous in our daily lives and one of the many minor inconveniences of technology. While many organizations are attempting to find better ways to authenticate users in the globalized age of the Internet, we generally accept that, although irritating, passwords are also necessary to protect us from attackers and to identify others across vast spaces.

Yet, passwords are far from perfect. Some systems, as we have already seen, can be brought down by a reel of thread. In fact, the basic hypothetical scenario that I outlined above contains within it a range of flawed assumptions.[2] The first and most basic of these is that a password might assist in identifying a *person*. In a world of high-speed automated cracking, it might just as well be a computer program attempting to convince the challenger (which might also be a machine) that it is actually a specific human or machine. A twenty-first-century robot vacuum cleaner might, either by trial and error or by software mapping, defeat the labyrinth.

The second assumption is that there must be an additional, already secret and previously established channel between the challenger and the respondent. In other words, it is necessary for *both parties* to know the password *in advance* and for this to be communicated without compromising its secrecy. Regardless of the form or route it takes, then, this 'second channel' implies that individuals must already be in communication with one another so that the secret word can be pre-shared. Passwords cannot identify people who are previously totally unknown to each other, at least via mutual connections. Passwords are also only useful after a time delay; they cannot be used before the second channel has secretly communicated the shared knowledge.[3] Passwords have their own temporality.

The third assumption, in the case of people authenticating themselves, is that a password must be capable of being remembered.[4] Although technological innovations such as 'two-factor authentication' can harden passwords against attack and beyond the bounds of human recall, many features of passwords are limited by the capacity of memory. As Aeneas Tacitus put it in the Roman era, passwords should 'be easy to remember'.[5]

The fourth assumption is that a password should identify a singular person. Historically and in the present day, this has not been and is not the case. Many passwords are issued to groups, such as armies, submarine commanders and so on. This greatly increases the difficulty of keeping the password secret and lowers the odds of detecting a misidentification.

The fifth assumption is that passwords might only help two people known to each other to verify that the correct individuals are present. But it is intrinsic to their nature that passwords can also betray. When a respondent gives an incorrect password to an enemy's challenge, he or she may be correctly identified as an imposter; an identification that is certainly not of benefit to the respondent. Conversely, if a respondent gives the correct password to a fraudulent challenger, the password will be compromised (for example, I might pretend that I know a password and ask you to tell me it, thus learning the true secret by deception).

Finally, I assumed in my hypothetical scenario that when the password is known by more parties than it should be, the error in identification lies with the challenger. If I ask for a password and a fraudster gives me the correct response, I might mistakenly believe the con artist to be someone else. This assumption has certainly shifted in recent years. In order to protect themselves, various institutions in the late-twentieth century displaced risk away from themselves and on to the authentic respondent in the eventuality of challenger misidentification. The term now used for such a failure to identify a remote party based on a password system is 'identity theft'. More commonly than not, there is an attempt to cast this as a fault on the part of the genuine user. This is a deeply flawed way of thinking about passwords.

These are just a few of the complexities that lie behind our contemporary systems of authentication. Despite the contrived nature of this example, however, it is also now clear that from the simple premises of passwords spring many difficulties and flawed cultural assumptions.

••••_

This is a book about the histories, cultural contexts and philosophies of passwords. It is a book about how 'what we know' became 'who we are' or how notions of identity have been culturally shaped by the evolving technologies of the password. Passwords are crucial to our lives. They regulate our finances, protect our communications and prove who we are to others. They are powerful words. But from where did this equation of knowledge with a person's (or a group's) identity emerge? What does it really mean, in the world of passwords, to say that one's 'identity has been stolen'? What does the future of the password hold in store? What actually *is* someone's 'identity'? And just how do we define a person?

Passwords certainly have a prominent place in many different historical contexts. For instance, most societies with a military presence have used passwords to restrict access. This was acutely developed in Ancient Rome, where an elaborate system of 'watchwords' was deployed that shares many of the characteristics of contemporary passwords (most notably, a secure second channel). 'Halt, who goes there?' is the canonical challenge. In addition to this, passwords appear prominently throughout literary history, such as in *Hamlet* when Francisco challenges Bernado to 'unfold' himself, but most often in the broader form of magical incantations. From the moment that Ali Baba overhears the magical phrase of the forty thieves – 'open sesame' – notions of secrecy and passwords are central to this well-known tale and its supernatural elements. Likewise, in more contemporary writing and film, the *Harry Potter* heptalogy is emblematic of pre-shared secrets uniting to give access to a hidden realm, be this in the more conventional passwords that grant students access to their Hogwarts common rooms or in the three-factor authentication of ability, wand and magic incantation (itself a type of password) that allows the bearer to perform a spell.

In more recent years, the development of digital cryptographic technologies and globe-spanning communication systems gave birth to the widest spread of passwords in human history. This stemmed from the fact that early computation was based on time-sharing systems in which there were 'multiple terminals which were to be used by multiple persons but with each person having his [*sic*] own private set of files'. As Fernando Corbató, one of the designers of the earliest time-sharing operating systems, said, 'Putting a password on for each individual user as a lock seemed like a very straightforward solution.'[6]

All of these instances of passwords, in fiction, film, militaries and the digital age, are like the labyrinth. They are all the same story of a challenge and response for knowledge that is supposed to identify people. Across historical periods the structure repeats, albeit sometimes facilitated and changed in form by technologies.

Yet, despite their widespread use, hardly anyone writes or thinks about passwords (except perhaps for computer programmers). Even Corbató struggles to realize the histories of passwords that made his choice seem 'straightforward' and obvious when he rhetorically asks, 'Surely there must be some antecedents for this mechanism?' Indeed there are and they are not just metaphorical references to 'locks'. But most writings about passwords are concerned only with pragmatic guidance for programmers on implementing or defeating software-based authentication mechanisms. The need for practical implementations of passwords has left philosophical and theoretical thinking at the starting gate.

••••_

What, then, is a password? What counts? What's in and what's out? While passwords can be used to protect access to spaces/places (restricted areas), knowledge (restricted communications) and actions (such as weapon launches on submarines), they also adopt these forms themselves. For instance, a password is often knowledge of a verbal formulation; a pass-word in its most traditional sense. They can also, though, take non-verbal forms that require an individual to act in a specific way: pass-actions. Giving the Masonic handshake is a 'password' (a pass-action) demonstrating shared knowledge. Finally, and most contentiously, a password can be a pass-space. As per my opening, a labyrinth that leads to a secret area, for instance, may require extensive geographical knowledge of its topology to be pre-shared.

As we've seen, a maze is not necessarily a very strong password because an adversary may be able to deduce the correct solution or find flaws in the security of the structure that allow the challenge to be bypassed. However, the same can be said of other forms of password. It was fairly easy to guess that my teenage brother's password to his computer would pertain to Arsenal football club, about which he was obsessed; it was 'Kanu25' (a player at that time followed by his shirt number). This is an example of the ease of deducing the correct solution. If I hadn't been able to guess the password, though, I might have been able to get in anyway by booting a different operating system from a CD ROM. This type of bypass of the password structure is more like Theseus's hack of the maze by finding a way to work around the test, rather than gaining the knowledge itself. In spatial contexts, the fundamental question then arises, however, of whether or not knowledge *of* a secret space is itself a password. The best example of this might be the hidden entrance to a prohibition-era speakeasy. The knowledge that one needs to enter is the location of the secret doorway (albeit perhaps with another password). Is this a password or just knowledge of where there is an entrance? Spaces are among the most difficult types of entity to classify and whether or not secret portals constitute discrete password systems is up for debate. That said, if a password system is boiled down in definition to shared knowledge that is supposed to limit the potential identities of individuals for purposes of authentication based on a challenge-and-response pairing, then it seems that some spaces can be classed as passwords, even if they are not strong systems.[7]

As readers will surmise, then, I take a broad definition of 'passwords' based on their function. Magic incantations, handshakes, mazes, the body and genetic codes are all phenomena that exclude or admit on the basis of pre-shared knowledge or ownership and that all contain an implicit or explicit challenge to produce these artefacts. Any object that excludes through the proxies of knowledge or ownership will be called a 'password' here because they are functionally identical to true pass-'words'. If we are considering passwords based on what they *do*, though, then it is important to seek the contexts in which they have most frequently appeared over history. After all, the uses to which passwords have been put are not invariant over time. However, given that so many passwords have been used to restrict access to military technologies of death, distinguishing allies from enemies, it is to this space that I will first turn. Speak friend and enter.

1 'WHO GOES THERE?': MILITARIES, MORTALITY AND PASSWORDS

Passwords are usually conceived of as keys to the lock of an identification request. A password traditionally protects access to something of greater consequence than itself (a space, a piece of knowledge or ability to perform an action) and can feel like the weak link in a system.[1] At their most basic, though, passwords are about shared *secrets* and/or exclusion based on identity. This notion of the 'secret' is crucial to a consideration of passwords. Without secrecy, there can be no need of a password. Secrecy itself rests upon concepts of exclusion and an inside/outside dichotomy. Those who know a secret are 'in the club', perhaps literally in the case of cult-like societies. Some spaces are more exclusionary than others, though, for a variety of reasons. Of the most secretive spaces throughout the history of humankind, few have been so restricted as militaries.

Militaries have used passwords for a variety of purposes over many centuries. Contemporary facilities, where militaries store weaponry that it might be illegal for civilians to possess, are guarded by complex systems of identity checks. Likewise in the present day, military computer systems clearly rely on password-protection mechanisms to prevent unauthenticated and unauthorized access to sensitive information and actions.[2] While these have evolved in complexity, they have been features of military life throughout human history. Indeed, as an immutable feature of military systems, passwords can broadly be categorized as protective objects across three different types of space: physical spaces, information spaces and action spaces.

Passwords, militaries and classical civilizations

Not every culture in human history has had a military. For instance, it was long uncontested that the Minoan civilization had no army, although the claim has come under scrutiny in recent years.[3] Likewise, the Moriori people of the Chatham Islands (Rēkohu) present a well-documented example of a totally pacifist society, which led to their eventual genocide at the hands of the Maori.[4] This is not to say that pacifist and non-militaristic cultures had no uses for passwords. Particularly in our digital age, there are many uses to which private citizens may put passwords. By contrast to these pacifist societies, however, we also know of cultures whose entire collective life and economy revolved around the military. Ancient Sparta is the best instance of this but claims for inclusion could also be extended to Britain in its period of high imperialism and the contemporary United States, according to critics of the so-called military-industrial complex. In fact, at the beginning of the twenty-first century it would be easy to posit a correlation between national political systems that result in economic strength and the scale of that same society's violence and warfare. One might even say, as does Jonathan Haas, that 'the economic and demographic conditions that are conducive to violence are also conducive to the development of complex, centralized politics'.[5]

Secrecy, which is the core component of passwords, is key to, but not determining of, successful, complex, centralized politics but also to cultures of coordinated violence. Obviously, secrecy is not sufficient to make a successful, complex, modern political system, even if it is necessary. There are many secretive regimes that fare poorly by most measures of success. However, even though secrecy is equated with corruption in strong contemporary democracies – a pathology of politics to which the likes of WikiLeaks pose themselves as the remedy – it is nonetheless true that 'modern states have not only built up massive, highly professional intelligence infrastructure' but that 'they also depend on espionage, secret operations, surveillance and the classification of information, which are indispensable governmental and military tools'.[6]

More importantly for the discussion at hand, 'secrets' take many forms and have different connotations and degrees of political legitimacy over time. Two of the most prominent types of secret that we can derive from classical societies are *arcana imperii* and *secretum*.[7] In ancient societies, as described by Aeneas Tacitus, the *arcana imperii* can be said to represent a withdrawal from knowledge. This refers to those moments when power deliberately takes the decision not to speak about events that would compromise its own authority. This type of secret then never has to justify itself or face any form of legitimation because it is unknown to those outside that there even *is* a secret. By contrast, *secretum*, which is far closer to our contemporary notions of secrecy, is a system of inclusion and exclusion. Under this mode, those who do not know the secret at least know that there *is* a secret, or they suspect it. This is a way of thinking in which there is a 'relation between the known and the unknown, between those who suspect and those who are "supposed to know"'.[8]

Passwords can fall into both categories of secret, but the second, *secretum,* is more common. It is possible, though, for passwords to take the form of *arcana*. If a particular body of authority, such as a military, decides to deploy passwords to control access but does not make it known that they have such a security measure, then this would be *arcana*. It is impossible even to think to crack or guess a password if you don't believe that the entity you are trying to defraud uses passwords. By contrast, in most cases that we encounter – and because the password is now so ubiquitous – many passwords are *secretum*. By this I mean that everyone knows or suspects that there is a password that will control access to military secrets, facilities and systems but only the select few know what the password actually is or the form that it takes.

This dual nature of the secret of the password and its importance in military history can be traced back to Ancient Rome and for a historical survey of the military password it is to this period that I will first turn. As an example of *arcana* consider that Tacitus counsels, in his advice on siege defence, that one should 'arrange in advance' for one's guards to 'communicate by whistling' in the event that they are separated, 'for this will convey nothing to those who do not know it'.[9] In this instance, the 'password' is the whistling that allows the identification of the individual. So far, so *secretum*. The important aspect to note, though, is that if the enemy does not know that this is the system of identification being used, they have no way of possibly impersonating those who do know the system. Thus, the military history of passwords is bound up in both *arcana* and *secretum*. In modern parlance, as I will come to later, these are analogous to 'security by design' and 'security by obscurity' respectively. Security by design is like *secretum*: everyone can know that there is a security mechanism and they can even know what it looks like and how it works. They still, though, cannot defeat it because knowing there is a password is useless if one does not know the password itself. By contrast, security by obscurity is like *arcana*. In this mode, insufficient on its own, an additional layer of hardening can be applied to a password system by ensuring that, in conjunction with a secure design, outsiders do not know what the mechanism is or how it works.

Aeneas Tacitus's historical military descriptions also show that, even in Roman times, the three core realms of password protection were evident: spatial, epistemological and practical (to do with place, knowledge and action, respectively). The first is the most obvious use of analogue password protections and pertains to the system of night watches that were established at Roman encampments. Tacitus prescribes that 'watches at night must be strictly kept in time of war and when the enemy are close to the city or camp' and that 'rounds and patrols should both demand the password'.[10] Clearly, this is a sensible precaution but it actually shares more in common with the problems of identification that I hypothetically raised at the very start of this volume. When identifying a soldier as friend or foe, it is crucial that this is done at a distance greater than the minimum range of that soldier's weaponry (a concept thoroughly alien in the contemporary world of globalized and potentially nuclear warfare). After dark in Roman times, this created conditions of distance and lighting that made oral password identification the only suitable and safe way of verifying identity claims. In other words, as with the contemporary situation, the password substitutes for a lack of facial or vocal recognition, whether this is because the parties are unknown to each other in that way or because a *distance* is imposed between the challenger and respondent, making this infeasible.

Tacitus also provides numerous examples of passwords protecting the epistemological realm (i.e. controlling access to knowledge) in Ancient Rome, mostly with respect to cryptography. Indeed, it is widely known that various figures in Roman times deployed cryptography, the most famous example being the Caesar cipher, named after the dictator of the Roman republic.[11] What is less initially clear is the role that the password might play with respect to cryptography.

Cryptography is the art of encoding messages so that only intended recipients can read them. It is usually an instance of security by design, as opposed to obscurity, in which it doesn't matter whether the communication can be intercepted, because the message remains unreadable. Besides the systems of asymmetric cryptography to which we will return, many systems of cryptography rely on the recipient knowing the word or phrase that has been deployed as a 'key' to the message: the password.

Ancient Roman and Greek cryptography, however, did not rely on passwords as keys in the same sense as we now conceive of them. All of the most prominent examples of ancient cryptography – the Caesar cipher and the Scytale device (a cylindrical tube that encrypts and decrypts by wrapping parchment around its outside) for instance – make use of shift or transposition ciphers, in which letters are either shifted by a set amount (for instance 'a' could become 'b', 'b' could become 'c', etc.) or transposed in a columnar fashion:

HELLO
THERE

becomes when re-aligned into columns:

HTEHLELROE

In each of these cases, what should be made known to a desired recipient is the method by which the encryption was performed. Since these ciphers are symmetrical, meaning that the same procedure is used to decrypt the message as was used to encrypt it, all the recipient needs to know is how the sender encoded their words.

In some sense, though, knowledge of the method of encryption (a kind of practice) might be a type of 'password'. Indeed, a restriction on knowledge of the method shares many of the characteristics of a password: it limits access based on a pre-shared system of knowledge. Restricting knowledge of the *practice* of encryption also demonstrates that the problem of the 'second channel' has been at the heart of password systems since time immemorial.[12] If attempting to send a secret message in Roman times, Tacitus notes that it is necessary that 'a private arrangement should be made beforehand between the sender and the recipient'; the second channel.[13] It is also clear that Tacitus's descriptions of passwords are sometimes to be accompanied by non-spoken components that, together with the oral password, make up one coherent item for access: 'A sign is sometimes employed as well as the password to prevent panics and for the better recognition of friends.'[14]

In one sense here, passwords that relate to cryptography are no different from other types of password: they give access to a previously inaccessible realm by verifying that the recipient is in possession of the pre-shared knowledge. It is simply that, in this case, the region to which the password grants access is itself epistemological (pertaining to knowledge) and communicative, rather than any physical space. From this example we can see that if the notion of a password in military history is extended to include non-oral components, as it is in Tacitus's formulation, then it is clear that cryptographic protection through secret methods (security by obscurity) is a type of password.

This is also the case with various forms of steganography that Tacitus lists. Steganography refers to another method for secreting communications, in this instance by hiding the message in plain sight. An example of steganography, albeit a weak one, is a sentence where italicized letters form the secret message: '*m*aybe *s*omething *s*omewhat *a*kin to *g*eneral writing' ('message'). Tacitus describes one way in which the ancient Roman military sent steganographic messages, with pre-shared knowledge of the method constituting the password that would verify the reader's permission to see the communication:

> A book or some other document, of any size and age, was packed in a bundle or other baggage. In this book the message was written by the process of marking certain letters of the first line, or the second, or the third, with tiny dots, practically invisible to all but the man to whom it was sent: then, when the book reached its destination, the recipient transcribed the dotted letters, and placing together in order those in the first line, and so on with the second line and the rest, was able to read the message.[15]

In other words, it is clear that passwords take many forms, especially when granting access to various forms of hidden knowledge.

Finally, passwords can grant permission to perform specific actions, particularly in military contexts. In the case of modern warfare, film depictions have made us familiar with the authorization codes that submarine commanders request in order to launch their nuclear weapons.[16] In the case of Tacitus's Rome, however, an incorrect password also served as an authorizing device to take a specific action. When Athenodorus of Imbros attempted to sneak into the camp of Charidemus 'they were discovered by means of the password'. Upon giving the incorrect (or no) password, 'some were driven out, others slain at the gates'.[17] In this context, action down two forks of a decision tree was authorized by a password, depending on whether or not the word given was correct.

Enigma: Complexity, calculation, making and breaking

Ancient Rome, along with other classical civilizations such as Greece, discovered the basic principles that underlie systems of authentication. These have not changed substantially even to the present day. What has changed over time, however, is the degree of complexity and calculation that is invested in securing systems of access to place, knowledge and action.

The best example of this link between technological development and warfare is the case of the Internet. As Janet Abbate, a prominent scholar of technology and science, puts it, 'In the years since the Internet was transferred to civilian control, its military roots have been downplayed. ... But the Internet was not built in response to popular demand. ... Rather, the project reflected the command economy of military procurement.'[18] Leonard Kleinrock, an American computer scientist who worked on the early form of the Internet (the 'ARPAnet'), likewise notes that 'every time I wrote a proposal I had to show the relevance to the military's applications.'[19]

This pattern of technological development following military application is well established and unsurprising. As just one further example, NASA's peaceful missions to space, for instance, are also underwritten by a distressing history. At the end of the Second World War, 'Operation Paperclip' was designed to bring the best Nazi scientists to the United States in order to further the rocket programme. The first head of NASA, Wernher von Braun, was one such scientist and there is little doubt that, had he not been useful, he would have been tried for war crimes relating to the slave labour of the V-2 project. As the old joke goes about NASA's links to the V-2 via von Braun: I aim for the stars, but sometimes I hit London.

In the case of passwords, wartime advances in technology come in two forms: in the development of new approaches and in the breaking of known methods. At the risk of a large historical leap forward from the preceding section on Ancient Rome, one of the most well known of these periods of advance came during the Second World War with the Axis development, and subsequent Allied cracking, of the Enigma machine.

The Enigma machine, recently re-inscribed in the popular consciousness by films such as *The Imitation Game* [2014], was used by the Nazis to send encrypted messages, especially during the U-Boat campaigns of the Second World War. The machine was a distinctive step forward in cryptography for its use of electro-mechanical rotors, although the approach taken by Enigma was not itself wholly novel. Indeed, the machine was based upon a fifteenth-century technique called a polyalphabetic substitution cipher. In a polyalphabetic cipher, each letter is shifted by a different amount depending upon the initial key. In the case of Enigma, the encryption key was determined by electrics and by mechanics, altering the substitution value on each letter-press from an initial setup state. This approach added an unprecedented level of complexity to the encoding keys (increasing the 'keyspace entropy', as it would be put in cryptography circles). Furthermore, the rotation of keys on a daily basis according to pre-defined cycles (the second channel) made it incredibly difficult to conduct cryptanalysis of the ciphers with any predictive force as it eliminated frequency analysis (the practice of observing that some letters, such as 'E', occur more frequently in the English language, for instance). Essentially, with Enigma, it did not matter whether one knew the mechanism; every day, the machine would generate a brand-new password (encryption key) that it was impossible to guess in any realistic timescale. Indeed, the US National Security Agency's analysis of the Enigma machine states that there were three novemdecillion combinations of potential encryption passwords.[20]

The particular case of Enigma raises an interesting aspect of passwords as they are used in contemporary cryptography: the aim is not to make a password unbreakable but rather to make it infeasible to crack a password within a meaningful timeframe. For the Nazi submarine operation, the complexity needed was as long as possible, but one day was clearly deemed the minimum (after which the rotors and wiring would be changed).

Despite what popular fiction and film would have us believe, Enigma was not 'broken' in any decisive, single move.[21] The cracking was also not the result of any single nation's or individual's effort (although, certainly, several great individuals were important). Finally, the ability to reverse-engineer Enigma messages was not achieved through the development of a single cryptanalytic method. While not as varied as the number of combinations afforded by the rotor mechanisms, deciphering Enigma was a fractured and diverse enterprise that demonstrates a range of approaches by which passwords are broken.

The earliest efforts at deciphering a three-rotor Enigma machine were undertaken by a Polish team and in particular Marian Rejewski, Jerzy Rozycki and Henryk Zygalski. Working off a commercial version of the Engima machine that they had purchased and in combination with information provided by a German traitor, the Poles were able to determine the wiring and rotor configurations on the Nazi Enigma machines. However, this would not let them read the messages because the initial configurations remained unknown. In order to deduce the rotor settings quickly, the Polish group built a machine (a 'Bomba') that could rapidly test the initial positions, allowing them to break the early Enigma codes.

In response to this, the Germans increased the capacity on their Enigma machines to a five-rotor device and it is at this point that the famous work of Alan Turing at Bletchley Park comes into the tale.[22] Turing was able to modify the design of the Polish Bomba to conduct a known-plaintext attack against Enigma messages.[23] In other words, Turing's device could eliminate impossible rotor settings by assuming that messages would include known phrases such as 'Heil Hitler', 'To' or, in the case of the first cracked Enigma message on D-Day, 'WETTERVORHERSAGEBISKAYA' (Weather Forecast Biskaya).[24] This was all well and good, but in the meantime the German navy had upgraded its stack of rotors to eight, from which they could select the three to be used. Without this knowledge, Bletchley Park could only read a very limited subset of messages. This headache for the Allies was then compounded by the addition of a fourth active rotor.

It was not until the capture of several U-Boats that the Allied forces, now joined by an American effort to build an array of high-speed Bomba-cracking devices, were able to modify their devices to take account of new rotors and the added complexity of a fourth rotor. In particular, the codebooks captured from U-559 were invaluable in giving a series of cribs against which the known-plaintext attack could be conducted.

This history of Enigma, presented above in an extremely condensed form, is well known and rehearsed. However, what it brings to a broader historical conception of military passwords is less frequently remarked upon. The introduction of electro-mechanical rotors into a symmetrical encryption process, all at a time of truly globalized warfare, began the era that extends to this day, a time when only machines can decrypt messages encoded by the passwords of other machines. The ways in which passwords can be broken in this era has some overlap with methods used in earlier times. For instance, it remains true that the simplest way to recover the encoded text is not through cryptanalysis or brute-force attacks run on complex machines, but rather to attack the second channel. If you can force your opponent to disclose the password, or if you can simply gain access to the shared secret, you need not try to guess it via machines. In this way, as the Web comic *xkcd* recently put it, in the imagination of a cryptography enthusiast, an opponent will be foiled by elaborate encryption. In reality, the opponent will simply physically assault the person who knows the key and extract the password, which is far easier.[25] This might be phrased as: if at first your attempts to ask nicely for the password do not succeed, hit your opponents with a heavy object until they reveal it.

Another way of thinking about the decision of whether to attack the primary or secondary channel is in terms of labour time. The complexity introduced by electro-mechanical devices raised the level of requisite labour to recover the password beyond those achievable by humans. In the case of Engima, the Allied crackers then built machine tools that amplified their labour power to levels that could determine the correct password. If, however, the labour power required to break the second channel is less than that required to build such tools or to guess the primary password, then an assault on the second channel remains the most effective form of attack. Passwords are only as strong as the weakest link, which in many cases are people and the second channel. Of course, there are usually stronger legal penalties for causing physical harm than for breaking into computer systems. This is designed to deter civilian criminals from assaulting people to recover passwords. In wartime, however, the situation is different and the state depends upon its legitimized monopoly on violence to attack the second channel.

Finally, the Enigma case study tells us something interesting about advances in password technology. At the start of this section I noted that progress in cryptography tends to occur more rapidly during wartime; whether in war or in peace, however, increases in complexity are often spurred by *breakage*. Put otherwise, the greatest advances in understandings of passwords are made not by those who encode messages or build systems of passwords. This group often believes that their systems are foolproof, uncrackable. It is only those who *break passwords* who bring the failings in authentication mechanisms to light. In this way, as the next section will explore, in the world of passwords, breaking is crucial to making.

Disclosure, militaries and the law

Let us return to one of the examples from the introduction to this book. In 2002, a Scottish citizen called Gary

McKinnon was accused by US government prosecutors of perpetrating the 'biggest military computer hack of all time'.[26] By the standards of individuals who might break into military computer systems, McKinnon was a relatively benign intruder. Exhibiting an obsession with UFOs, free-energy-suppression conspiracy theories and supposed antigravity technology, the uncovering of which was his sole declared motivation in invading military systems, he was later diagnosed with Asperger's syndrome and the UK government controversially blocked his extradition to the United States. Unlike many accomplished computer crackers, however, McKinnon did not gain access to the US military's systems by writing exploit code that turns a computer program against itself. Instead, as we have already seen, he simply automatically scanned for blank passwords on US government computers. Finding their password system deficient, he ended up with wide-ranging access to a number of sensitive networks. To make an analogy with locks: the US military didn't put any on its doors.

To continue this story, the US government's response to the breach was swift. McKinnon was threatened with up to seventy years in prison under allegations that he had deleted key files on military servers. To some, this seemed reasonable. After all, if McKinnon really had crippled the national security systems of the United States, then this was something that must be deterred in future. On the other hand, if US military password security was really so poor, then should not the government be thanking its lucky stars (and perhaps McKinnon) that this was brought to their attention, even if inadvertently? After all, seventy years is many, many more times the length of a prison sentence that would be given for a physical assault; it's more akin to an espionage sentence.

The issues raised by the McKinnon incident form the final case study that I will here draw from military histories of passwords, pertaining to issues of 'responsible disclosure' and legality. By way of background, these problems have long been grappled with in computer-security circles. If one finds a vulnerability in a piece of software, how should one disclose it to the software's creator? One camp of security experts claims that security vulnerabilities should be disclosed in secret to the software maker. The argument here is that, in such cases, users will be protected because the findings will not be made public. This rationale does not, however, stand on particularly solid ground. For one, malicious adversaries may have independently discovered the vulnerability, in which case users are unaware that they are at risk. For another, it is unclear what incentive software companies have to fix software if they (erroneously) believe that a problem is trivial and that nobody will ever find out about the bug.

This aspect of security disclosure practices was described well by Bruce Schneier, a renowned authority in the field, who wrote:

> To a software company, vulnerabilities are largely an externality. That is, they affect you – the user – much more

than they affect it. A smart vendor treats vulnerabilities less as a software problem, and more as a PR problem. So if we, the user community, want software vendors to patch vulnerabilities, we need to make the PR problem more acute.[27]

Schneier instead advocates for the norm to be 'full disclosure', where vulnerabilities are detailed in full, in public. This, obviously, exposes users to danger from attackers. The halfway, moderate point that most researchers use is called 'responsible disclosure', where the threat of full disclosure is backed by an embargo period; the software developer is given the information privately for a limited time period in which they can fix the bug before the vulnerability is made totally public.

What has all this got to do with passwords and militaries? In fact, quite a lot: state militaries depend upon societal legitimation to hold a monopoly on violence. If militaries are shown to be incompetent with respect to password security, then the public will feel unsafe. Without public backing, militaries lose their legitimacy. The question then becomes about what we value more highly: the legitimation of our national militaries or true public safety.

This can be seen, albeit with some complexities, in the McKinnon case. McKinnon discovers a large number of default passwords on Internet-connected military machines. Clearly, this is a huge embarrassment for the military; a massive 'PR problem' as Schneier would put it. However, the military also has a conflict of interest here. Of course, the military would like the public to think that it is entirely internally secure and competent, but this is clearly not the case. The military then has to balance two opposed logics. On the one hand, public safety would be increased if the military invited researchers to attack their password systems and responsibly disclose problems when found (malign opponents are already trying this, without the disclosure, so there's less of a risk). On the other, the military's legitimacy will be eroded with every disclosure as public confidence in its competency is diminished. In other words, military password systems can only embrace the strengthening power of breakage at the expense of their own existence and legitimation.

In McKinnon's case, it is clear that the military felt extremely threatened by the PR disaster, which is why such lengthy prison sentences were proposed. McKinnon was not, strictly speaking, a 'white-hat hacker', a term that describes hackers whose sole aim is to disclose vulnerabilities responsibly. His motivation was not to disclose the information he found to the authorities. However, McKinnon was also hardly the most dangerous of felons. As the rise of information warfare continues, it is clear that militaries face a double bind in their duty to protect the public and in their mission to continue to exist. Where they should draw the line at prosecution is unclear, for while a legal deterrent seems logical, it will only deter those with a wish to obey the law that is stronger than a desire to break into military systems. Hardened criminals and foreign governments hardly fit in the first category, while a range of individuals with the expertise to expose problems do.

•••• _

What can we say, at the close of this chapter, about the philosophy of passwords that was less clear before? First, militaries have been core users of passwords throughout human civilization. Defending access to technologies of death remains an important use towards which passwords are put. There are two different types of secret that derive from ancient definitions into which passwords can be categorized: *arcana* and *secretum*. Passwords are more commonly of the second type, *secretum*. Passwords protect access to realms of space, knowledge and action in different contexts. Passwords are linked to cryptography, allowing access to knowledge in this field. The complexity introduced by electro-mechanical inventions in the twentieth century pitted machine against machine in the battleground for authentication and decryption for the first time. However, devices such as Enigma, and other systems of passwords in general, are rarely cracked in one fell swoop. Breaking passwords leads to the formation of stronger password systems in the dialectic of making and breaking, of creative destruction. Finally, militaries in most contemporary societies are dependent upon government and popular legitimation. Opening their password systems to the scrutiny of this making/breaking dialectic can lead to the decline of their support base. At the same time, by closing off this valuable channel of expertise, they weaken their password systems and do not gain the full benefit of breakage.

It was not the intention of this chapter, though, to suggest that militaries are the sole drivers and users of passwords. Indeed, when we return to digital passwords in Chapter 3, it will become clear that civilian uses are of great importance. In anticipation of that discussion, however, we will now turn to the ways in which passwords have been represented in literature and religion to make clear the extent to which they have permeated our society over their long history.

2 SPECIAL CHARACTERS: PASSWORDS IN LITERATURE AND RELIGION

The cultural influence of passwords can be clearly seen when one considers that perhaps the most important canonical work of English literature – William Shakespeare's *Hamlet* – depicts authentication in the first three lines of the play. As the curtain rises, the night-watch guards Barnardo and Francisco encounter one another in the dark. Barnardo demands to know 'Who's there?' to which Francisco responds, 'Nay, answer me. Stand and unfold yourself.' Francisco's counter-challenge implies his authority by saying, no, I will not identify myself, identify yourself, thereby flagging the problems of mutual identification and the potential to reveal passwords to unauthorized persons. Once Barnardo has successfully identified himself (using the less-than-cryptic password, 'Long live the king!'), their discussion can proceed and, conveniently, the pair actually recognize one another as individuals, thereby skirting the thornier problem of how Francisco could identify himself.

The presence of passwords in this play is, however, not so surprising. In one sense the password exchange between Barnardo and Francisco is merely another reflection of the military environment. After all, Shakespeare's tragedy is set within the militaristic contexts of the Danish royal court and Elsinore castle at this point. What we are given, therefore, is an accurate depiction of the military use of passwords: dramatic mimesis. Shakespeare draws on the audience's expectation of military passwords use to create a credible environment. Yet there is so much more to the use of passwords here because identity and verification, as embodied in Francisco's challenge, are absolutely core to the thematic preoccupations of *Hamlet*. For one, we can see the way in which the password moves from *arcana* to *secretum* at the moment that Francisco challenges; the announcement that there is a password system in place. More importantly, though, the misconstrual of identity sits at the centre of *Hamlet*'s plot. It is, for instance, the misidentification of Polonius as Claudius that leads to the death of the former at the hands of Hamlet. It is also significant that Polonius is the spymaster of all roles, the character whose job is most concerned with dissembling and misrepresentation. Likewise, while Polonius is still living, he has a lengthy conversation with Hamlet in Act III, Scene II, about the polymorphism of the clouds, playfully suggesting first a camel, then a weasel, then a whale, which forms a powerful metaphor for misidentification and shifting forms. No, the password at the opening of Hamlet is not merely a detail added for the sake of realism; it is a crucial device for the entire play. It is both first and central.

Many hundreds of thousands of words have been spilt in the analysis of *Hamlet* and I do not propose, here, to inflate their ranks; we would gain but a little patch of ground/That hath in it no profit but the name. Indeed, while *Hamlet* does give an opening into the world of passwords in literature, it is a very *conventional* type of password that appears, an expected rendition of military procedure, even if thematically core. What will be of more interest to readers, I hope, are the instances that follow in which I trace unusual ways in which passwords are used in literature, indeed ways that can *only* be accessed by works of fiction. Primarily, this realm of passwords that is exclusive to literature pertains to magic.

Passwords, myth and magic

In Anglo-American cultures, the most famous tales from the *Arabian Nights*, or *One Thousand and One Nights* as it should properly be called, are 'Aladdin; or, The Wonderful Lamp', 'Ali Baba and the Forty Thieves' and the seven narratives pertaining to 'Sinbad the Sailor'. As legacies of imperialism go, this is a fairly damning statement given that these tales were not Arabic originals but were actually inserted into the *Nights* by a Frenchman, Antoine Galland.[1] In particular, it is clear that 'Ali Baba and the Forty Thieves' – the specific tale to which I will shortly turn – was transcribed by Galland from a conversation in March 1709 with a Maronite scholar, Youhenna Diab, before Galland then interpolated the story into the *Nights*.[2] In this light, we must take care, then, to note that inferences drawn about passwords from Ali Baba are perhaps more reflective of eighteenth-century imperial France and Europe than of first-century Islamic cultures.

This warning aside, the tale of 'Ali Baba and the Forty Thieves' presents one of the best-known instances of passwords in early literature. Few English speakers have not heard and would not comprehend the story's central phrase, 'open sesame', even if they could not pinpoint its original source. The tale's narrative is familiar: Ali Baba overhears the password used by a gang of thieves to gain access to their secret den and himself enters, stealing a single bag of coins. Upon learning of the cave, Ali Baba's brother, however, is greedier and intends to take a larger quantity of loot. Tragically, the brother is trapped in the cave and the thieves return and brutally murder him. When Ali Baba then removes the body for burial, the thieves are alerted to a security breach and try to track down the eponymous protagonist. Thanks to the cunning and ruthlessness of his slave girl, Morgiana, Ali Baba is saved from the thieves' attempts to kill him and ends the tale as the sole possessor of the secret password to the cave.

Ali Baba's tale begins, simply enough, with a classic representation of passwords. The thieves arrive at the designated place and give the 'strange words' that will identify them. When the thieves have left, Ali Baba correctly realizes that a system of passwords exists (now *secretum*, not *arcana*) and that he may be able to fool the authentication system by giving the same words himself. The thieves, upon detecting the breach, attempt to harden their mechanism by killing all those who might also know the password and by displaying their bodies as a deterrent to others (an extreme form of making from breaking). Where the story differs from military passwords and other real-world instances is that the words are magical and the entrance appears out of nowhere in response to the incantation. It is not a human or even a machine demanding that others identify themselves, but rather a supernatural force or being that controls access.

Magic is not bound by the laws of physics and reality, of course. However, literary representations of magic usually gain credibility through an identifiable non-magical analogy. A good example of this need for a real-world connection can be seen in flying broomsticks for witches, which have been present in literature since at least 1489. This trope takes a familiar object (a broom or a stick) and, using magic, renders that object analogous to other forms of transport. Likewise, fantastic beasts are often described by their relation to other animals with which we are already familiar: centaurs being a combination of horses and humans, for example. Such a comparative approach is necessary because the human capacity for imagination, although wide, is not unbounded. People tend to imagine the future in metaphorical terms that pertain to the present, hence at the turn of the twentieth century the first automobiles were referred to as 'horseless carriages'. The need to relate the new to the present has strong precedent and good writers will not introduce something (either futuristic or magical) that cannot be imagined by analogy to a reader's familiar reality, even if the author's aim is to de-familiarize that reality.

FIGURE 2 A scene from Ulrich Molitor's *Von den Unholden und Hexan* (circa 1489) showing hybrid beasts and broomsticks. Image out of copyright (public domain).

This explains why the precise depiction of the password in *Ali Baba* lies somewhere between passwords as we have seen them so far and a new form. What we actually see here is a password where, as before, there is a second channel; the thieves know the password in advance, thereby making it possible for them to enter the cave. However, what is different is that the second channel is completely magical, presupposed but impossible to find or attack. We do not know when or how the supernatural force or being first communicated the password to the thieves.

Interestingly, though, *Ali Baba* also reveals an aspect of passwords and knowledge that we haven't yet broached. The tale of 'Ali Baba and the Forty Thieves' is only possible because the password is an object of knowledge that can be transferred. The original thieves, by the end of the tale, are all dead but the password remains active and working. This is a situation involving what we might refer to as a 'non-rivalrous object' and it is one of the reasons that the term 'intellectual property' remains contentious.[3] Non-rivalrous objects are objects that can be given to, or taken by, another without the original copy being lost. Non-rivalrous objects are contrasted with traditional material objects. If you take my keyboard, I will no longer have it; the object was contested for ownership because only one copy existed in physical space.

Knowledge and digital items are not like this. Multiple people may have the 'same' idea at the same time and it does not follow that the first person lost the idea. This is inherent in the other tale of the *Nights*, Aladdin, where the protagonist discovers the pass-action of rubbing the lamp to release the genie. He was not the first or the last to have the idea to rub the lamp and multiple figures may know the secret without others relinquishing their knowledge. In this instance, of course, one must also *have* the lamp: property combined with knowledge. Interestingly, the concepts of copyright and intellectual property are designed to refashion artificially and limit non-rivalrous objects so that they can work within a rivalrous market based on material scarcity and money through the law. In other words, we legislate to treat non-rivalrous objects as though they were rivalrous so that they are compatible with our systems of finance (which are rivalrous – you can't have my money at the same time as me or the entire system will break down because we will both spend it). In the digital space, in which perfect, instantaneous copying is possible, many traditionally rivalrous forms become non-rivalrous: music, text and images, for example.

Another fairy tale/magical password environment demonstrates this thinking further. In the tale of 'Rumpelstiltskin', as collected by the Brothers Grimm, a mischievous imp helps a young girl to fulfil her father's overambitious boast that she can spin straw into gold. Saving her life in the process, the imp-like character eventually demands the girl's first-born child as payment, an element of her promise on which she later wishes to renege. The imp agrees that she may avoid her debt on condition that she can successfully guess his name. The imp knows that this is extremely unlikely as his name is 'Rumpelstiltskin'. Nonetheless, the girl comes across the imp singing to himself in the forest, overhears him saying his own name and, the next day, successfully delivers the word that will redeem her.

The tale of 'Rumpelstiltskin' is one of many worldwide variants of the so-called 'Name of the Helper' myth, according to the Aarne-Thompson classification system of folklore.[4] In fact, this pattern of tale, in which the name of an individual acts as the key, is utterly pervasive throughout many cultures and it reveals two facets of passwords that are relevant to the discussion here. First, there is a striving in this tale for the word of power to be connected directly to identity. No word is more personal to an individual than his or her name. To make this word a secret – as is also seen in other areas of popular culture, such as *Doctor Who*[5] – ties a secret system of knowledge (passwords) to identity. Secondly, as I have been arguing, a name-as-password is a powerful demonstration of the way in which passwords are non-rivalrous forms of knowledge, for the tale is hugely contrived. What is the point of a name but to allow others to identify themselves? In using a name as a password and thereby keeping it secret, one is using a form that is supposed to be disseminated – to be copied and 'owned' by others even while the originator also knows it – with a totally artificial restriction.

This reveals an interesting contradiction at the heart of many types of passwords, namely that authentication mechanisms are systems of rivalrous exchange built upon non-rivalrous objects: passwords. This dense statement can be unpacked with some ease. When we design systems of authentication – designed to prove someone's identity –

we *need* those systems to be exclusionary. It is absolutely intrinsic to their nature that they are able to distinguish, based on shared knowledge, whether a person or a group is the presumed bearer of that knowledge. For this to work the knowledge must be unique to the person or group; it must be exclusionary and rivalrous. But the system that we use, in many traditional circumstances, is based on knowledge, which is a non-rivalrous form. Many people can know the same thing without the original person losing the knowledge, although the power or capital of the knowledge may be degraded by its ready availability. A secret is only worth as much as its keepers' discretion. However, this contradiction of needing falsely to economically limit a form (knowledge), as per the tale of *Ali Baba*, sits at the conflicted heart of passwords.

Harry Potter and the two-factor authentication device

But magic will find a way. Indeed, if one wanted to search for a series of works wherein a variety of magical passwords are depicted that demonstrate the range and diversity of such systems, one could do worse than to consult J. K. Rowling's *Harry Potter* series. Works of fantasy have long depicted passwords in many forms. For instance, J. R. R. Tolkien's *The Lord of the Rings* famously presents a riddle challenge to the

Fellowship at the Doors of Durin – 'Speak friend and enter' – to which the correct password is 'friend' in Tolkien's fictional Elvish language, Sindarin. Yet few works in the present day have given so much space to different types of password as *Harry Potter*, be it in the text's magic incantations, the students' common-room passwords, access to the Chamber of Secrets via parseltongue or the blood-password of the 'weakness payment' to the Horcrux Cave. Some readers will, of course, baulk at drawing conclusions about a serious technological and social object, the password, from works of children's fiction. On the other hand, it pays to remember that Rowling's series is, as of 2015, the best-selling set of books of all time. If one cannot draw conclusions from the most widely disseminated works of contemporary literature – not to mention the film adaptations – then from where could one?

For those unfamiliar with the narrative, the *Harry Potter* series charts the adventures of the otherwise normal, young eponymous orphan protagonist who discovers that he has magical abilities. As his years of study at Hogwarts School of Witchcraft and Wizardry progress, the tales turn darker while the war with the dark wizard, Lord Voldemort, moves to the foreground. Unfolding over the course of seven books, published over a ten-year period from 1997 to 2007, and eight films, from 2001 to 2011, the series was the first major publishing success of the twenty-first century.

Passwords, even when not billed as such, are integral to the universe of Harry Potter. Indeed, by just the first few dozen pages of the first book, *Harry Potter and the Philosopher's Stone*, the reader has been introduced to three security systems that protect spaces: the entrance to The Leaky Cauldron, the entrance to Diagon Alley and the entrance to Platform 9¾ at King's Cross Station.[6] Each of these depends, in some way, on pre-shared knowledge in order to gain admittance. For instance, The Leaky Cauldron, a public tavern, is nearly invisible to all but the wizards, a group who already know of its existence. Likewise, the entrance to Diagon Alley, the wizards' high-street, is guarded by a wall that can be opened by tapping the bricks in a specific order. Both of these instances of 'password' (or pass-action) are *arcana*; most are unaware that a secret even exists. Finally, for this first appraisal, though, the case of the entrance to Platform 9¾ is the most interesting. At this point in the text, Harry Potter is given instructions to board the train from this platform by Rubeus Hagrid. However, Hagrid neglects to share, in advance, the requisite knowledge (the 'password') to enter the platform space and so Harry has to conduct a 'side-channel attack'. While, of course, Harry is not unauthorized to enter the platform (i.e. the character is not a malicious intruder), he is unauthenticated at this time and adopts a similar approach to any other attacker of a password system. Walking around the platform, the character listens to the conversations of others until he hears how the system works, information that can then be used to his advantage.

Other instances of spatial-access-control systems abound throughout the *Harry Potter* novels. Some are extremely simple and consist of spoken words to enter places, the most obvious examples of which are Dumbledore's office, the student common rooms and the prefects' bathroom.[7] Two other aspects of Rowling's world, however, gesture towards the fact that magical passwords in literature can circumvent the weaknesses of traditional passwords in reality. This is shown in the world of Harry Potter, where it is not always enough to know the password. Instead, one must actually *be* someone.

The first of these transformations towards identity and away from simple knowledge is seen in the entrance to the Chamber of Secrets in the second *Harry Potter* book. In this novel – which most strongly begins the series-long parable of racial prejudice – a monster is released into Hogwarts School to hunt down those of supposed 'impure' bloodlines, a legacy of one of the school's founder's racist views. The location whence this monster came remains unknown for most of the book, but it is speculated to be a mysterious chamber beneath the school. Finally Harry Potter finds the chamber and gains entrance by speaking the supposedly straightforward password, 'open up'.

However, all is not quite so simple. To gain admittance to the Chamber of Secrets, one must say the words 'open up' in a mysterious snake-language called 'parseltongue'. Throughout all of the *Harry Potter* books, including the canonical (but non-main-series) *Fantastic Beasts and Where to Find Them*, Rowling mentions only seven individuals capable of speaking parseltongue.[8] In other words, parseltongue serves as a severe restriction on who can gain entrance based on *who someone is*, not just what it is they know. This is because parseltongue is not, according to Rowling, like an ordinary language. In a 2007 interview at Carnegie Hall, Rowling explicitly stated, 'I don't see it [parseltongue] really as a language you can learn.'[9] This resembles no other meaningful language on Earth as all languages must be acquired by speakers at some point in their lives. Rowling's magical language is different, though. In her universe, the language parseltongue (if it really can be called a language) is an innate part of a person's genetic (or perhaps wizarding) constitution. Harry Potter only possesses it because of his strange connection to Lord Voldemort in which they share each other's psyches. It is true that Ron Weasley is able at one point to replicate a single syllable of parseltongue in order to himself open the Chamber of Secrets. For all intents and purposes, however, parseltongue is not about what you know, it is about who you are – an important shift in thinking about passwords.

It is clear, then, that works of fiction can use magic to move towards 'utopian' systems of passwords, by which I mean systems that do not rely on proxies of knowledge for identity but rather give un-mediated access to identity. For this is the utopian, perfect state towards which passwords strive: to erase themselves as intermediaries and to somehow purely represent personhood. We can see this utopian urge once more with an example from *Harry Potter*, indeed, the most fundamental of plot elements in these books: magic itself. To cast a spell in the world of *Harry Potter* – as in many depictions of magic – one must know the incantation.[10] There is a secret, shared knowledge of a word that must be communicated beforehand (a second channel) that allows one to perform the action of magic: '*stupify*', for example. But it is not enough to know the password in this case. As with the Chamber of Secrets, to cast a magic spell, one must also *be someone*: a wizard or witch.[11] So far, nothing is new here. However, in Rowling's universe there is a final component in the system that protects access to magic that relies on *having an item* as well as knowing a word and being someone: a magic wand.

Ostensibly, the wands in the *Harry Potter* series are a crucial component for the performance of magic. The wands contain, we are told, magical artefacts ('dragon heartstrings' as one example) that somehow channel the wizard's ability. Yet they also clearly serve as an authentication system. Near to the end of the series, in a trial scene, a character is accused of not really being a witch but simply of having stolen a real witch's wand. Likewise, a major plot element of the final novel centres on whether the Elder Wand can identify its master and properly serve the correct witch or wizard. Magic wands seem as though they are mere amplifiers of innate ability. I contend, though, that they are actually what we might call multi-factor authentication devices, a way of enhancing security by deploying multiple proxies for identity at the same time.

Multi-factor authentication will be explored more thoroughly later. What I want to close with here, however, is the observation that magic and passwords seem tightly coupled to one another but in complex ways. Why does Rowling have to ensure that her witches and wizards need an object to limit access to magic when it is clear that one must already be a magical person? Objectively, she does not. However, by replicating systems that we now use to mitigate the weaknesses of passwords in her fictional realm, Rowling makes clear the central ethical theme of her books: determining people by any kind of identity, race or supposed inner essence is problematic and difficult. Identity categories are fluid and, in the racist world of *Harry Potter* where those of supposed lesser parentage are discriminated against, Rowling seems to be saying that we are unlikely to see radical change in the world until we acknowledge this. The way in which she chooses to complicate this identity/knowledge split in her works, however, is through passwords.

The Word

The final and strongest instance of ideal-state passwords in the *Harry Potter* novels, then, is the act of casting magic itself. More broadly, though, there is a long list of literary texts, religious beliefs and other cultural artefacts that tie the practice of magic to verbal incantations. In a way, as the final part of this chapter will explore, this links the ability to access specific practic (pertaining to action) and epistemic (pertaining to knowledge) spaces directly to identity.

Perhaps the most well known of these is the Christian Bible's Gospel of John, where the very first line of the very first verse reads, 'In the beginning was the Word, and the Word was with God, and the Word was God.' Despite the fact that 'the Word' clearly refers to Jesus (as the 'Word of God' made flesh), this has also been interpreted, by many commentators, as instigating a logocentric metaphysics in the Western world, a worldview in which the Word is the privileged mediator of reality (things are known and understood via words).[12] This verse of John is significant, however, because it directly echoes and supplements Genesis 1.1-3: 'In the beginning God created the heavens and the earth. Now the earth was formless and empty, darkness was over the surface of the deep, and the Spirit of God was hovering over the waters. And God said, "Let there be light," and there was light.' In this mode, God is both the Word and uses the Word to create the world. The Word precedes the world and fills the formless and empty void with light and substance. In this tradition, God speaks the Word that is equivalent with himself and through this has the power to create the universe. This is perhaps the most powerful and secret piece of knowledge ever ascribed to the utterance of a word that is directly tied to a being's identity, the password to end all passwords. It is also not surprising that it set a bad precedent in password practice: the first password was the world's birthday.[13]

Other ancient cultures have different types of supernatural passwords that give access to power. In many of these cultures, deciphering (or cracking) divine signs and passwords gives access to power and knowledge. Indeed, in the Akkadian language of Ancient Mesopotamia, the word for 'omen' is the same as 'password'.[14] This dual meaning at once causes an interesting overlap between interpretations of god-given signs and passwords, for both are systems that presuppose shared knowledge. To be privy to the machinations of gods, one must be versed in reading the omens; a second-channel of training in and learning of these sign-systems must be in place. Having access to the divine mind, clearly, bestows power.

For just one more instance of this phenomenon, one can consider the Ancient-Egyptian *Book of the Dead*. Geraldine Pinch notes, of hieroglyphs in Ancient Egypt, that 'the power of the image and the power of the word are almost inseparable'.[15] This power is clearly seen in the remarkable inscriptions found in the *Book of the Dead* that are supposed to guide the dead spirit safely to the afterlife. In other words, a series of spells are given, in advance, to the deceased, the knowledge of which will grant him or her access to a supernatural space. Of course, the spells are highly restricted as one must be dead for them to work. One must also have been of a social class with enough wealth to have a funeral in this style. Nonetheless, this brand of magic once more ties identity much more tightly to knowledge than is possible in a physical, as opposed to metaphysical, realm.

For this is the major shortcoming of passwords, as they exist in our real world: they don't really verify who someone is, they verify that the respondent knows something. Works of literature based on systems of magic, such as the *Thousand and One Nights* and the *Harry Potter* series, allow authors to construct a reality where these shortcomings are mitigated. The tale of *Ali Baba* shows a situation in which there is no original second channel and so the depiction of passwords is immune to second-channel attacks; the password has always somehow existed. At the same time, the story shows the weaknesses in real passwords when they are intercepted. By contrast, the *Harry Potter* books depict a series of passwords in their conventional form and then juxtapose these with more utopian, ideal systems of magical passwords that do not rely on the respondent's knowledge, but instead directly recognize the respondent's identity. Finally, tales such as 'Rumpelstiltskin' show the way in which this striving is achieved. By using a *name* as a password, the inherent flaws of the distance between words and identities are revealed. Literary, cultural and religious interactions with magic and the supernatural often act to bridge the shortcomings of passwords, as they actually exist.

3 P455W0RD5 AND THE DIGITAL ERA

Digital technology and the Internet have many effects on the contemporary world. One of the most lauded, however, is the perceived collapse of space and time. In the twenty-first century, it no longer takes weeks for a message to arrive on the other side of the world, even if the continued demand for low-cost international flights indicates that we do still favour in-person contact. But the digital age has changed not just spatial distance but also the very way that we use mixed metaphors of space to refer to non-physical artefacts.[1] Hypertext websites, for instance, are 'visited' (they are, by their very name, 'sites'). Online discussion functions are called chat-*rooms*. Indeed, a plethora of spatial metaphors has been deployed to refer to the virtualized *environments*, *forums*, *spaces*, *places*, *sites*, *rooms* and *home* pages in the digital *world*.[2] Yet, even if these digital phenomena are conceived of as places, they are also spaces of knowledge, often based upon text and reading; they are *pages*, e- or Face- *books* and communications. Finally, however, digital environments are also places of action: we *surf*, *scroll*, *click*, *enter*, *log in* and many more. In short, the ways in which we linguistically frame digital technologies – and particularly the Internet – pertain to the three areas in 'real-life' that are protected by passwords: spaces, knowledge and action. It should be no surprise, then, that with the growth of the digital, we would see the re-application of passwords as the means of determining identity and controlling inclusion and exclusion.

As of 2016, almost the first requirement imposed upon any user of a modern computer system is to enter a password. As our lives become ever more digital, the need to restrict access to online resources for reasons of personal privacy and property is intensified. This is part of what Alan Liu has charted as a contemporary 'unreal hunger for security' that corresponds to an unlimited and perhaps opposed desire for connectedness in the information age. As we become more connected, our information systems by necessity become easier to access, both by authorized and unauthorized users. In fact, there cannot be an increase in connectivity (which is about access) without a commensurate decrease in security (which is about access restriction). The best security is to unplug the computer from the Internet. The 'enter password' screen has become, then, part of the security-theatre apparatus that appeases our need for connectedness with a counterposed theology of unlimited security. 'Enter password' is the core iconography of the religion of security and restricted access in a world of mass inter-connectedness.

This is, though, a 'metaphysics of security' and, for Liu, passwords are our 'oaths to transcendental security'.[3]

However, mathematical and computer-scientific perspectives on the password that were introduced in the latter part of the twentieth century do fundamentally change the concept of shared secrets.[4] In the contemporary age, the mechanisms involved in security have moved towards publicly known processes or algorithms that produce publicly known results. In the present day, a respondent to a challenge must produce the single piece of input knowledge that will create the correct output when put through such a process, not the final output. This relies on the development of one-way, irreversible algorithms and a notion of asymmetry previously unseen in passwords: only one person knows the secret. In this contemporary environment, Theseus's symmetrical thread attack on the labyrinth would not work. It is no longer possible to use the same route in to escape. This begins the era of one-way streets, the time of asymmetry.

Cryptographic hash functions

The clearest way in which to begin this exploration of digital asymmetry is through a description of cryptographic hash functions and the most simple of the problems that they solve for passwords. In all systems of passwords, the reader will recall, it is necessary that the secret knowledge of the password be pre-communicated to the relevant parties. In a computing environment this means that the remote system must store a copy of a user's password so that, when a user provides the secret word, the system can confirm whether or not it is correct. Unlike the magic scenario of Ali Baba with its supernatural entrance ritual, there is a determinate place where a computer is storing your password whenever you login so that it can be checked. In contrast to a human-to-human interaction, though, when computers store information it is susceptible to interception by others. After all, if the computer can read it, technically it might be possible for others with access to the computer to do likewise. This means that, if the password is stored in plain text, anyone who violates the system will have permanent knowledge of the passwords of all the users on that system, a far-from-desirable situation. Like the wizards attacked by mind readers in the world of Harry Potter (a 'Legilimens'), computers are vulnerable to external penetration. Along with other defences, this is where systems of cryptographic hashing enter the equation.

A cryptographic hash function is a one-way algorithmic process that takes a *message* and produces a *digest*. To put this differently, this is a process that can take any piece of input text and produce output text that *uniquely represents* but is *different from* the input. If the process is run multiple times with the same input, it will generate the same output. It is also supposed to be impossible to recreate the input text (message) from the output text (digest); it is 'one-way'. For instance, in the Message Digest 5 (MD5) algorithm, the message 'object lessons' yields the digest '1d67a7d36f9be2e642bd3bd3fc14071a' every time. It is clear that the output bears no resemblance to the input. What may be less apparent is that it is supposed, in this algorithm, to be impossible to deduce that 'object lessons' was the input if one only knows the digest '1d67a7d36f9be2e642bd3bd3fc14071a'. If I give you only the message digest '495b3e607e3eaf05d987ac81ba6cd0d5', you are never going to know the embarrassing personal message that it contains – I hope. This is because the digest is not an 'encryption' of the message but is more like a fingerprint; it uniquely represents, but is not equal to, in any way, the finger. In fact, in this algorithm, the digest does not contain all of the input; parts of the message are deliberately discarded so that it is impossible to go back to the original.

Thinking of this as a form of *language* reveals just how strangely radical a break this is. Indeed, like Parseltongue, this is among the most curious types of translation ever devised. Imagine a language that one could only translate *into* but never translate *from*. In this imaginary language, every time you translate from English (for example) it is totally clear and unambiguous what the translated text should look like. There is no room for judgement, only precision. And yet in this language it is impossible to translate back to English. It is not that we could only approximate the English equivalent or that we might be unsure exactly which word we should use; there is no possibility of recovering the corresponding text. This is a language and mode of translation unlike any other in human history and it is a very good analogy to cryptographic hash functions. In another way of thinking about it, with reference to the mythological labyrinth with which I began, this is like a maze where with every step you take the floor behind you drops away. Or perhaps like the house in Mark Z. Danielewski's extraordinary novel *House of Leaves* [2000] where the internal spatial configuration of the property mutates behind the explorers. The route takes you closer to the centre but you can't go back.

So, how are cryptographic hashes actually used if the computer doesn't know the original password? Surely this makes it impossible to verify whether a response to a password challenge is correct? The 'language' and its 'translation' appear useless. Not so. Instead, the computer re-hashes the user's input at the time of login and compares the hashes. Because the algorithm produces the same output every time and runs extremely quickly, the computer can simply process the user's input and check if the hash at the other end is the expected result. It is true that this 'language' is useless for communication. But it turns out to be very useful if you want to check whether somebody knows the same thing at a later point in time – the very same deferred temporality common to all passwords.

The idea behind this method is that, even if an attacker has the stored hash, he or she will not know the user's password, which means that if a user has the same passwords for access to multiple services, he or she will be safe. None of this is to say, however, that there aren't attacks against cryptographic hash functions.

The easiest form of attack against cryptographic hash functions – but not necessarily one that will succeed, for reasons that will shortly become apparent – is a brute-force attack. This consists of sequentially trying every possible combination of input passwords until the hash that matches is found. For a ten-character password, however, including spaces, uppercase and lowercase letters, numbers and special characters, there are 60,510,648,114,517,025,000 password combinations. On a mid-range consumer PC as of 2016, it would take about 220 thousand years to try every combination for the MD5 algorithm.[5] This impossibly long timeframe is why it is a good idea to use complex passwords. If an attacker can be sure that the original message is a common word in a dictionary, he or she can simply use a list of words, thereby substantially reducing the time required to break the password.

Of course, one way in which this attack can be accelerated is to pre-compute all of the potential values and to store them in a database for speedy lookup (the process of searching is much faster than the operation of computing the hashes). In the language/translation analogy, this would be like creating a dictionary for the one-way language, except that it's not just a 'dictionary' of words, but has to be a dictionary of every possible set of letters in every single possible combination. At that point, it becomes infeasibly large.[6]

The second type of attack – one that is far harder to execute but that reveals a more fundamental flaw in the system of cryptographic hash functions – is a collision attack.

This consists of finding two input messages that generate the same digest. In the imaginary language scenario, this would be the equivalent of the English words 'cat' and 'dog' both translating to the same word in the imagined language. It is supposed to be impossible, in a securely designed hash function, for this to occur. However, in reality, over time attackers often find ways of generating multiple input messages that will match an output digest, which severely degrades the security of such an algorithm.[7] Theoretically, this means that an attacker could use a different password but still get access to your account.

Feasibility studies and designs of the first cryptographic hash functions did not come about until the late 1970s and, in many ways, they instigate a new way of thinking about shared secrets.[8] Following the post-war advent of the discipline of computer science and the ensuing uptake of mathematical approaches to cryptography and security, the assumption that now underlies this particular use of cryptographic hash functions is that the second channel is pre-compromised. In other words, the knowledge that is pre-shared is no longer sufficient to fool an identity verification system that is based around a mathematical operation/process in which the input cannot be derived from the output. My embarrassing secret message remains safe.

Fearful asymmetry

While the use of cryptographic hash functions in the verification of passwords is an important and useful development in security, this particular use pales into insignificance when compared with the discovery and implementation of public-key cryptography, also known as asymmetric cryptography. Until these algorithms were developed, all systems of passwords were, in one sense, symmetric. It was necessary, in all preceding historical systems of passwords, for the secret to be communicated to all parties so that they could identify themselves or decrypt messages.

This outdated thinking of passwords as symmetric remains the way that passwords and encryption appear in much popular culture. In the (fairly terrible) film *Swordfish* [2001], for example, Hugh Jackman's character Stanley Jobson is forced to hack into the US Department of Defense under a set of coercive and 'distracting' circumstances.[9] Despite the fact that Jobson is using code at this point, supposedly to circumvent the 'enter password' screen, the visual representation of this process is a typical password-style dialogue where Jackman's character fails on his first few attempts to correctly guess the access key. On the final attempt, he succeeds, with this plot device echoing the familiar experience of dread at the ATM when the third incorrect entrance of a PIN may mean an account lockout. Hacking prowess is depicted as a type of three-strikes-and-you're-out process wherein the pre-communicated shared secret must be deduced.

You will probably not be surprised to hear that these representations do not reflect how most systems of contemporary cryptography and authentication work. The visual metaphor of the password remains a powerful way to quickly depict processes that have little to do with entering a secret word. In asymmetric systems there are two keys required to send a message. One key is made public and can only be used by other parties to *encrypt/send* messages. In other words, if you want to send me a secret message, you would encrypt your communication with my public key. The other key is kept secret by the person receiving the message and can only be used by him or her for *decryption/ reading*. You encrypt with my public key, I decrypt with my private key.

There are two interlinked ways that asymmetric encryption procedures can be used to verify identity, ways in which they become systems of passwords and ways in which they replace the type of authentication seen in films such a *Swordfish*. The first is via a simple message relay. If I send a message to Alice, encrypted with her public key, that says 'hello', and

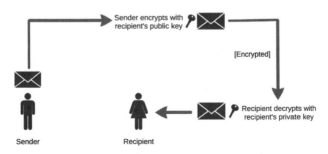

FIGURE 3 An asymmetric encryption and decryption process.

the person claiming to be Alice can tell me what the message said (because she possesses the private key), then I can be certain that I have got the right person.[10] Except, as with all systems of passwords, that certainty is slightly misplaced and confuses the map with the territory, the proxy with identity. Assuming the integrity of the asymmetric algorithm holds, what I have really proved is that the person to whom I sent the message has access to the corresponding secret key that will decode the message. In this instance, the proxy is not conceived of as knowing something (since private keys are too long to remember) but having something. This no more proves that somebody *is* someone than any other form of password.

The second way in which asymmetric encryption can be used to prove identity arose in response to this problem: the idea of 'certificate authorities'. Certificate authorities are third-party mediating entities deemed to be 'trusted' by a large community. The role of a certificate authority is to attest that a public key belongs to a specifically named subject. This is designed to get around the problem specified above: that asymmetric cryptographic techniques prove possession, not identity. With the addition of a certificate authority, a trusted third party asserts that there is equivalence between possession and identity.

There is, though, something interesting going on around the discourse of trust and identity here. One of the ideas of public-key cryptography is that it might foster greater trust through transparency and through third parties vouching for others. In a culture of total transparency and openness, it has been argued, there will be more trust.[11] But this relies on a curious logic. In a culture of trust, there is no need for transparency. If I trust my spouse, I will not demand an itinerary of her, like some jealous lover. By contrast, it is in cultures underpinned by suspicion, conspiracy and paranoia that these demands for transparency come in. It is wrong-headed to think that by demanding that public-key certificates be openly presented and that certificate authorities attest to their validity that we have created *trust*. If we did not *distrust*, if we had no belief that there was malice 'out there', we would have no need of such systems.

Public-key cryptography, then, which thrives in a culture of paranoia and distrust, has nonetheless proved remarkably resilient to attack. The mathematical logic on which most asymmetric systems rest is that it is computationally infeasible to prime-factor large numbers and no trivial algorithmic process exists for such a process. (And I mean here *really* large numbers, over one hundred digits in length.) So long as this remains true, asymmetric encryption techniques will persist. However, like any other system of passwords, encryption or security, asymmetric cryptography is only as secure as the weakest component that protects it.

In reality, there have been several instances where certificate authorities have been hacked, although none, so far as I am aware, by Hugh Jackman or John Travolta.[12] In this type of incident, the third party can no longer be trusted and may falsely assert that a key belongs to an individual. Because the assumption is that the certificate authority proves that an individual *is* a specific person if he or she is in possession of a key, if the certificate authority is compromised and this remains unknown to me, I might give restricted information, the right to perform restricted actions, or access to restricted spaces to a fraudulent attacker. Certificate authorities are, therefore, a problematic weak link for asymmetric encryption keys.

Likewise, the private key file must be stored on a computer as it is too long for a user to remember. This presents an additional attack surface. If an attacker can find another way to compromise the machine on which the private key is stored – such as a social engineering attack where one might pose as an IT engineer in order to obtain the user's regular password fraudulently – then the system of 'trust' is also silently compromised. Some mitigation against this particular attack (compromise of the private key) is offered by encrypting the file with a password. In one sense this is a form of multi-factor authentication; it requires the user to 'have' something (the private key file) as well as to know something (the password to it). In another, though, this is only a quasi-multi-factor system. This hinges upon the fact that digital 'ownership' is not identical to property.

Although, above, I noted that the asymmetric key system looks like a shift from knowledge to ownership, it's actually slightly more complex than that. The security of many asymmetric key-based authentication systems is, in fact, dependent upon a somewhat flawed conception of unique digital knowledge as analogous to physical property. Private key files, which can be 'stolen', are protected by passwords even as they are, themselves, a form of password. This isn't true multi-factor authentication, though, because one doesn't 'own' the private key file (it is a non-rivalrous digital object that can be copied *ad infinitum* even while the premise of secrecy rests on exclusive access). Unlike ownership, it is more appropriate to say that one 'knows' the private key file, having delegated the remembrance of a complex and long number to a computational device. The actual security of such a system, then, depends upon hardening a digital memory against external penetration.[13] This is a bit like property – it depends on protecting exclusive access – but the object of protection is actually more akin to knowledge. The metaphor in computing that consists of referring to volatile and non-volatile storage media as 'memory' is, therefore, extremely apt but far from perfect.

This type of thinking brings us back full circle to where I began this chapter. The difficulty in thinking about immaterial objects – like passwords and keys – through a language that has grown with notions of ownership most suited to rivalrous physical property (spaces, places, rooms, sites) has implications for passwords. You may own the storage media (hard disks, DVDs, etc.) on which a password or asymmetric key resides but does that mean you own the key itself? What does it mean to say that you 'own' an 'object' that can be copied indefinitely with total fidelity? A couple of examples from copyright law will better illustrate the difficulty. First, consider the case of a photograph that one has recently taken. This is probably a copyrightable expression and so you have the right of ownership under law. Even if you display this photograph publicly and allow thousands of people access to see it, online or physically, and regardless of how many copies exist, you still have a legal right that is analogous to 'ownership' of the photograph. By contrast, let us say that you have owned a photograph for the entire term of copyright (for argument's sake, it was once published but is now impossible to find due to obscurity and destruction of the original publication). Once the copyright has expired, you will have no legal right of ownership over reproductions of the photograph but you will still have access to the only version, meaning that nobody else can make a copy. This phenomenon, whereby two types of ownership – physical ownership and legal ownership of an item that can easily be copied indefinitely – overlap, is exactly the same for the type of security surrounding asymmetric encryption keys. You can try to protect physical access to the media on which the key is stored, but this does not necessarily mean that adversaries do not possess copies of the key. Likewise, you can try to protect the idea/content/expression of the key through legal and technological means but this will only be as effective as the physical and network security of access. I will return to these problems of property and knowledge in the next chapter.

The era of asymmetric encryption and passwords is part of a broader move towards a science and mathematics of passwords. Without the fundamental theoretical mathematical work and then computer-scientific implementation of those algorithms, these mechanisms for authentication would not be possible. As I indicated at the start of this chapter, however, in many cases we use metaphors to think about the outputs of technologies that do not really have direct physical analogies. The implications for the philosophy of passwords extends into metaphors of memory, property, knowledge, space and ownership and this is seen nowhere so clearly as in asymmetric key-based encryption.

Biometrics

The most recent development in the realm of passwords at the time of writing pertains to the use of biometrics for authentication. This can be seen in the fact that several technological media outlets have published approving, but I would suggest pre-emptive, articles framing a 'plot to kill the password' through biometrics.[14] As the term implies, biometrics refer to the measurement (metrics) of organic matter (bio). The rationale behind these technologies is that we might dispense with using knowledge or possession as proxies for identity and skip directly to measure a person's unique genetic constitution (with identical twins being the exception) and its expression in physical features (such as fingerprints, retina, iris, face, voice). As usual, though, this is hardly straightforward.

One of the most widely cited works on biometrics suggests that there are seven core elements to which the designer of a biometric system must attend: universality, uniqueness, permanence, collectability, performance, acceptability and circumvention.[15] Universality refers to the fact that all users of a biometric system must have the biological elements to be measured. If it is possible that users do not have hands, eyes or other body parts, then a system that measures these will be insufficient. Uniqueness is the condition of specificity; the aspect to be measured must be different from all other people. Permanence refers to the fact that people's biological elements change over time; a biometric system requires a relatively stable item to measure. Collectability means that the item to be measured must be capable of being collected with proportionate ease. Performance refers to how well the system is able to use biological measurements to determine identity correctly. Acceptability refers to the degree of positive social response to the idea (whether people baulk at having their eyes scanned, for instance). Finally, circumvention is the term used to denote the ease with which the system might be compromised.

There are two main uses to which biometrics can be put: authentication and identification. Up until this point I have treated these two terms as roughly synonymous but there is, in fact, a subtle difference between the terms. Authentication occurs when a specific individual is matched to a single identity. The question asked in settings of authentication is whether a person present can produce a matching biological pattern for one particular set of information that was previously stored. Identification, in the context of biometrics, works slightly differently. In a biometric environment, identification means searching a database for the information that correlates to a specific individual. In other words, authentication is a one-to-one process: Does this unique individual before me match the information I have on file? By contrast, identification is a one-to-many operation: Which of the many records that I have on file corresponds to this individual? 'Is this person the right person?' versus 'Who is that person?'

Biometric technologies are interesting with respect to the asymmetric age of twenty-first-century passwords. In some senses, biometric approaches are symmetric. If an attacker can find the pattern stored for someone's iris, for example, he or she may be able to create a replica of the eye that will fool a scanner. Indeed, the first batch of eye scanners could be fooled by holding up a picture of the correct eye while early face scanners could likewise be fooled by an image of the corresponding face. In this sense, usually due to technical defect, biometric implementations seem to be symmetric.

However, at the same time, when implemented correctly, biometric technologies are asymmetric. In theory, it shouldn't matter whether you know that my eye will open a door because we do not have the ability to create bespoke organic matter. This may change, of course, as genetic engineering advances, but for now, biometric authentication systems rest upon a simple premise. Information, including organic information, about an individual may be public and an attacker will still not be able to bypass a correctly designed biometric system.

This is not to say that hypothetical, often violent, situations have not been envisaged to defeat biometrics, even when the authentication systems are technically sound (i.e. they require a requisite body to be present). These instances of body-part removal in order to gain access have primarily come from literary and film contexts and are referred to, by the well-known Wiki *TV Tropes*, as a 'borrowed biometric bypass'.[16] Dan Brown's *Angels & Demons* and Warner Bros.'s 1993 film *Demolition Man*, for example, both give instances where a psychopathic character removes an authorized user's eyeball in order to defeat biometric iris scanning. In the case of *Demolition Man*, the specific grisly moment occurs upon the escape of Simon Phoenix (played by Wesley Snipes) from cryogenic prison. Phoenix uses a ballpoint pen to gouge out the eye of a prison warden that he then holds up to the scanner in order to break free.

FIGURE 4 Simon Phoenix deploys a grisly borrowed biometric bypass in the film *Demolition Man*. Copyright Warner Bros. 1993. Used under fair-dealings provisions.

With respect to the philosophy of passwords that I have been tracing – noting an equation of knowledge or possession with identity – the biometric bypass is of particular significance. The fact that body parts might be transferable entities has considerable implications for the definition of identity and self. Indeed, in these cases, body parts become just another transferable item that can defeat an authentication system and identity cannot, as such, be part of any link to a body. Bodies become conceived of as mere property and not integral to identity by evildoers who wish to bypass biometric security systems.

Other cinematic works have used borrowed biometric bypass tropes in a more metaphorical and nuanced way. The 2002 film *Minority Report*, for instance, weaves a complex relationship between knowledge and the body. In the world of this film, which is based loosely upon Philip K. Dick's 1956 short story of the same name, murders are seen before they occur by three 'precognitive' beings, allowing the police department to arrest perpetrators before the crime has been committed. The plot takes an unusual turn in that the chief of police, John Anderton (played in the film by Tom Cruise), is predicted to commit a murder about which he knows nothing in advance.

As with most films that deal with foresight, one of the key themes of the movie is free will; does knowing one's eventual destiny yield the possibility for change? What is perhaps less clear to the average viewer, however, is the degree to which the body is the key authentication device in the film. One instance of this is obvious. The future world of *Minority Report* is saturated with eye scanners. In one gruesome moment, the protagonist has his eyes surgically removed and a fresh pair re-inserted so that he can adopt the identity of 'Mr. Yamamoto' and move around the futuristic city without being detected. However, Anderton keeps his old eyes in a bag so that he can use them to gain access to sensitive areas (revealing a fairly gaping hole in the plot: Surely such access would have been immediately rescinded?).

More subtly, however, the main narrative of the film revolves around the dual thefts of a single body in order to gain access to knowledge. It transpires that the man who built the system that allows the precrime unit to see into the future had to have the mother of one of the 'precogs', Agatha, murdered. Anne Lively, Agatha's mother, wanted her child back. This was unacceptable since Agatha's precognitive abilities were crucial to the precrime system. In this way, Agatha's body and mind are stolen so that the precrime unit can have access to knowledge of the future. As Yari Lanci puts it, what emerges 'is a constant struggle for the monopoly over a pre-emptive grasp of the future'.[17] This 'pre-emptive grasp of the future' is pre*cognitive* – that is, a mental process pertaining to knowledge and thought – but access to it is monopolized through control of the *body*. Agatha's body in the film *Minority Report* acts as a biometric (organic), psychometric (psychological) and psychimetric (psychic) access key to the monopoly of the pre-emptive grasp of the future.

The second theft of a body in order to gain access that occurs in this film, however, is part of the main narrative. After being accused of murder, Anderton wishes to ascertain whether he has a 'minority report'; a rare occurrence in which one of the precogs sees a different future to the other two. However, the precrime system in *Minority Report* requires protection against false positives (where a crime is wrongly forecasted). As one of its inventors in the film notes, 'For precrime to function, there can't be any suggestion of fallibility.' For this reason, these minority reports are destroyed and stored, for the record, 'inside the precog who predicted it'.

Anderton therefore undertakes to steal the precog Agatha from her nutrition tank, modifying his face via a powerful drug so that he can enter the compound and not be detected. As he tells her, he must do this because she 'contains information'. In a mirror of the fact that Agatha was originally stolen from her mother, the nutrition tank from which Anderton 'steals' her in the film is notably shaped like the female reproductive system. Most importantly, though, the theft of the body by Anderton is to gain access to information; the body allows the violation of the mind in this world. Agatha is once more reduced to a body that can be used to gain knowledge, an item of property to be stolen, in contrast to the intention of biometrics to bind agency, personhood and self purely to the body.

FIGURE 5 The precognitives and their womb-like tank in *Minority Report*. Copyright Twentieth Century Fox Film Corporation 2002. Used under fair-dealings provisions.

The questions that are raised by biometrics and the ability to bypass them are about the nature of human selfhood. Passwords in previous eras were concerned with the ways in which knowledge might act as a proxy for identity. Proving that one had access to pre-shared knowledge in some form was the best that could be hoped for in systems of authentication. Then, around the 1970s, the mathematicization of passwords began to complicate notions of ownership and knowledge. The question became one of protecting access to a material space (a hard disk, a networked computer system) that could potentially be violated by an adversary in order to gain access to knowledge stored in a virtual 'space': the externalization of memory. Finally, the idea was that if knowledge was inadequate and if these external sites of storage were also fallible, perhaps linking identity directly to someone's body might work.

Except it doesn't. A person's body may change and yet they remain the same person. The borrowed biometric bypass trope also demonstrates, at least in horrific theory, that the body may be mutilated in order to fool biometric systems. On the other hand, someone who suffers brain damage in an accident is, again, still the same person. He or she may no longer be able to remember information that we might use for authentication, but his or her core personhood remains. I do not mean, by 'core personhood', that there is some kind of natural, unchanging essence to a person. People are the result of a complex set of interactions between their genetic constitution and the environment that surrounds them and change over time. Instead, I simply wish to point out that a person can recognize another person both as a human and as an individual in an intuitive way that seems to defy the formalization that we seek in systems of passwords. In other words, authentication mechanisms – and particularly those that rely on technology – attempt to use a set of proxies (knowledge and the body) to identify people. These proxies, though, are insufficient. People are neither solely their bodies nor just their brains. They are not even simply a combination of these aspects. More than in most other phenomena, passwords, mathematics and biometrics continue to show us, even as secularization marches onwards, that we still seem to have no viable definition of a human, of a person. Some call this object that we seek and fail to formalize a person's 'essence'. Others use the words 'personhood' or 'self'. Still others call it the soul.

4 IDENTITY

It is clear by now that passwords are not simply mechanisms of identification and authentication. Instead, in their various forms, passwords expose a broader set of problems concerned with human identity, knowledge and the body. Passwords are also revealed as instruments of exclusion from spaces, knowledge and practices, while themselves taking these forms. In this final section, we will more thoroughly explore the ways in which notions of identity are bound up with the problems of passwords. In particular, I want to draw attention to the rhetoric of 'identity theft', a formulation that only became possible with the emergence of a specific conception of passwords. Namely, at a certain point in the rise of the digital technologies, situated amid the creeping rise of a universal language of economy, passwords became so seemingly natural that organizations operating with sensitive information online – often financial institutions – became able to claim that knowing the same thing as someone else *makes you that other person*. In reality, what seems to be meant by the phrase 'identity theft' is that a malefactor is able to use knowledge to illegally take on the societal roles rightfully belonging to someone else, such as accessing a bank account or claiming social security benefits. The discourse of identity theft is only possible, therefore, in a world where a person's 'identity' is conceived as little more than the sum of his or her functions in society, functions to which an individual has access only because he or she is supposed to uniquely know certain things. This is the bold assertion that sits behind the words 'identity theft'.

'Theft' in a non-rivalrous world

In Chapter 2 we saw, through various forms of literature, how passwords need the quality of exclusion. If more people know the password than are supposed to, then the system has been defeated. At the same time, however, we also discussed the fact that passwords often take the form of knowledge. As above, knowledge is a non-rivalrous object form, meaning that it can be copied indefinitely without the originator losing access. In order to consider what it might mean to have one's identity stolen, then, I suggest that it is first imperative to understand what we mean by 'theft' in the digital age, which involves a little more thinking about the nature of knowledge and property.

Resuming the discussion begun in Chapter 3, the artificial legal notion of intellectual property has been sustained in recent times by rhetorical analogy between unauthorized reproduction and theft. There is, though, a crucial distinction between the terms. Theft is the act of dishonestly taking someone else's property and therefore depriving them of access to it. In UK law, for instance, it is quite explicit that to steal something means the original owner loses access: 'A person is guilty of theft if he dishonestly appropriates property belonging to another with the intention of permanently depriving the other of it.'[1] US law varies from state to state, but all larceny-theft provisions are divided into two components: (1) dishonest appropriation of property; (2) with the intent to deprive the original owner of it.

This becomes important in cases where anti-piracy groups seek to make an analogy between theft and unauthorized distribution of their copyrighted material. For instance, the infamous 2005 campaign, 'Piracy: It's A Crime', was spearheaded by the Motion Picture Association of America and made such a link explicit. 'You wouldn't steal a car,' the announcement began, before continuing, 'You wouldn't steal a handbag / You wouldn't steal a television / You wouldn't steal a movie / Downloading pirated films is stealing / Stealing is against the law.' And yet, by the laws of most countries, copyright violation is a civil, not criminal, offence and it is certainly not stealing. Importantly for the point that I am making here about passwords, by downloading a pirated film, one does not deprive an original owner of property. It is true that these acts of 'piracy' might make it harder for the copyright holder to profit from the work in future, but this incalculable future speculation is difficult to include in consideration of present property under theft statutes.

Downloading is an act of copying in which a new party gains access to something even while the original owner continues to have that same object.

Indeed, it is difficult to think about theft in a digital world, even when it comes to *money*. In previous eras, when money was a physical item such as a banknote or coin, the only ways to obtain more money illegally were to either fraudulently forge a copy of these items or to steal somebody else's coinage. In the digital age, things are different. 'Money' is often simply a numerical representation, stored within a computer system. This has led some to note that the legalistic definition of theft is perhaps out of step with the needs of a digital world of infinite reproduction. Jaron Lanier, for example, uses this aspect of digital currency to argue that if we believe that downloading is not 'theft', because it doesn't deprive a specific other of property, then the same might be said for someone who 'hacked into a bank account and just added money'. This is confused metaphorical thinking, though. Lanier is right that what a criminal would have violated here is the law of the 'artificial scarcities that allow the economy to function'.[2] What is wrong is to turn this back into theft. It is, instead, directly analogous to minting one's own new currency fraudulently, in contravention to the social and legal contracts that forbid this: theft versus fraud.

Passwords (in line with all other digital and knowledge 'objects') are not like physical property. Knowledge cannot be stolen. It can be taken and copied without permission but this is not theft in any legalistic sense. Why, then, does the term

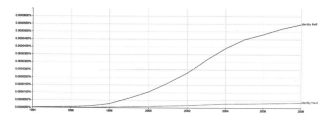

FIGURE 6 The rise of 'identity theft' as the preferred term to denote the circumvention of password mechanisms as seen in the Google Books corpus, 1994–2008.[3] Used by permission of Google: https://books.google.com/ngrams/info.

'identity theft' so clearly begin to outperform the alternative formulation, 'identity fraud', from the late 1990s onwards? Clearly, an identity cannot be stolen, in the true sense, any more than the proxies that we use to denote it (a password). Indeed, 'identity fraud' is a much better term. 'Unauthorised access' would be even more accurate. But it is identity theft that has become the term that is used. Why?

Identifying risk

I contend that the reason that the term 'identity theft' is favoured over any of the alternatives is that it absolves institutions in the digital world of responsibility for the inherent flaws in their authentication systems. In turn, by displacing risk, these institutions are able to offer convenience to their customers as a trade-off against security. The way in which this displacement of risk works can be seen in a systematic analysis of the different phrases that we might use to describe such forms. Throughout the following analysis it is important to remember that online authentication systems are standing in as long-range systems that are supposed to fulfil a social function: to establish trust on the basis of identity. That they have weaknesses should not be used as an excuse simply to avoid the difficult questions of blame, risk and fault when these weaknesses are exposed. At the same time, however, as consumers we often want the convenience of long-range access while also wanting security, two aspects that are usually pitted in trade-off against each other. Passwords and the online systems that surround them are so common to us that we now tend to think of them as natural, as though they are the only and best solution to the problem of identification. This is dangerous, though, since we can end up with a situation where the password systems that we have are deemed perfect and it must be people who are to blame – and particularly the person who is to be identified – when they are circumvented. Before proceeding, I do want to note upfront that in the case of financial institutions, which feature as my primary examples in the following section, a bank will usually refund your money and take the risk themselves (sometimes for public relations reasons, sometimes due to regulation), even while using the term 'identity theft'. I contend, though, that this might change in the future with the normalization of the idea of identity theft as a linguistically valid concept.

If, then, the phrase used was 'unauthorised access', the immediate question becomes: Who gave authorization and how is this different from authentication? In the scenario of someone hacking into my bank account, for example, it is clear that I have not authorized the user to perform any actions on my account. As a general rule, I tend to restrict the right to redistribute my own money to myself. And yet, probably through some compromise of my password, in this hypothetical situation a user has managed to persuade the bank's authentication system that he or she is me. In turn, this technological mechanism may then authorize the hacker to undertake actions on the assumption that it is I who is acting. In this scenario, the phrasing implies that something has gone severely wrong in the institution's process. I did not give authorization and so am not to blame. The bank's authentication system was not good enough to distinguish between me and an attacker and so made an error. From this error of authentication, the system (and by implication the bank) made an additional error in then authorizing this user to take actions that I have not in any way sanctioned. From the perspective of a financial institution, 'unauthorised access' is about the worst of the list as it makes the error almost entirely that of the bank.

Conversely, if the phrase 'identity fraud' is used, then the role of an institution becomes slightly different. While still having made a mistake in identifying a person, institutions here become victims. The error, in other words, is neither the fault of the end-user nor entirely of the bank. Indeed, the phrase 'identity fraud' quite clearly places the blame upon the act of duplicitous impersonation. While there are steps to be taken against being defrauded, this is certainly more favourable to institutions whose compromise might involve financial loss since it implies that they should be less liable for the outcome. On the other hand, though, cyber-criminals are notoriously hard to track down and so it is very hard to summon a real, concrete figure to blame. The other interesting mutation that has occurred around this term, though, is the frequent claim that it is end-users who are the victims of fraud and not the bank.

This is, itself, curious. One would expect this when the term 'identity theft' is used; after all, the victim of the theft is the person losing the stolen 'object'. Why, though, have those impersonated been cast as victims of fraud in this discourse? Turning once more to legal definitions, fraud by false representation occurs when someone has 'made a false representation, dishonestly, knowing that the representation was or might be untrue or misleading, with intent to make a gain for himself or another, to cause loss to another or to expose another to risk of loss'.[4] Yet to whom has the false representation been made in the example scenario that I have been using? It is certainly not the user who is being impersonated. It is, indeed, extremely unlikely that I would fall for a scam in which somebody falsely claimed to be me. Identity fraud can, logically, only have a victim who is someone other than the person being impersonated! Instead, continuing the banking example, it is the financial institution's authentication mechanism that has been tricked. And yet, for many years now the discourse of identity fraud has been mutating towards one that attempts to make the person impersonated the victim. Certainly, the person impersonated may suffer as a consequence, but it is important to note that he or she is not the party who made the misidentification.

The re-situation of blame in online password structures towards a system where it is users, not institutions, who are at fault, finds its highest form in the term 'identity theft'. The discourse of 'digital hygiene' (which refers to regularly changing passwords, running anti-virus software, etc.) has it that, as with poorly secured items in the physical world, users should take personal responsibility for their identity or property.[5] Indeed, most insurance policies for theft in the 'real world' require that the policyholder implement a set of precautions to protect the property themselves and any lapse may invalidate a claim, thereby recentring blame on the individual. The same goes for passwords in the rhetoric of identity theft. Rather than conceive of password systems as flawed and weak, most banks have clauses that protect them from litigation if the user takes insufficient steps to protect the pre-shared knowledge. Although this formulation of 'identity theft' is technically nonsensical, then, as I have already pointed out above it is also attractive for institutions. If the general public can be made to believe that the inherent weaknesses in passwords are not actually flaws but it is rather that their identities have been stolen (because they practised poor digital hygiene), then this softens the way for banks and other authentication providers to change their liability provisions at a later stage.

The fundamental appeal of the logic of identity theft lies in its direct analogy to physical property. Relatively few people can understand the technological workings that sit behind complex systems of authentication. By representing technology through metaphors of the physical world (i.e. by making it seem that the technology is a transparent translator of the physical), it is more likely that existing thinking will be applied to the technology. In doing this, authentication providers hope to re-apply existing legal logics in the virtual space. But the virtual realm does not behave entirely like the physical world and the conflation that is sought is multiple: physical property should be thought of as analogous to knowledge which in turn should be considered analogous to identity. The core shift in thinking that this flattening logic entails is that, in the digital age, what you know is to be considered as who you are. Knowledge and identity are inseparable.

Knowledge/Identity

In the past thirty years of thought in the academic humanities, few formulations have been so widespread as Michel Foucault's notion of Power/Knowledge. Most clearly articulated in *Discipline and Punish* but furthered in his *History of Sexuality*, the notion of Power/Knowledge is not the same as the clichéd formulation that 'knowledge is power'. It is instead an observation that power is based upon monopolizing the right to specify how truth and knowledge are understood. Foucault uses the example of the religious confession as an example of this. In a confession, the penitent is told (power) to produce statements of truth (knowledge) about his or her forbidden desires. This then forms a feedback loop as the knowledge that is produced empowers the confessor to absolve the penitent of sins.[6] In Foucault's history, aspects of confession leaked into psychiatric practice during various phases of secularization. In this way, psychiatry employed (and in Foucault's reading, continues to employ) the power of confessional truth speaking to *produce* various forms of subject identity that must then be controlled.[7] The other core example of this is the power now bestowed upon scientific practice. While it may seem incontrovertible that science aims towards truth, such a statement was not accepted throughout human history. In previous eras there was no empirical science, as we know it. At some core point in our recent history, however, the discourse of experimental repetition and intersubjective validation ('science') became the primary custodian of truth (with just cause; its advances are admirable). Often, as Umberto Eco points out, this emergence of empirical science was contentious and could not be understood as truth because it conflicted with other forms of stronger social truth and meaning, such as the Bible.[8] Thinking about science in this way does, though, empower a type of truth-producing practice (discourse) that is not universal and absolute, but historical and relative. More importantly, it is not that power and knowledge are identical but rather that they demonstrate interchangeability, a close co-dependency.

Passwords interact with this truth/knowledge problem because they are technologies of power that produce identity through knowledge and bodies. They are *technologies* because they are the formalized and routinized tools and implements through which we exclude. They are technologies of *power* because they are used to regulate and control access. They *produce identity* because, in the moment of utterance or performance of a password, an individual classifies himself or herself in the eyes of another, usually into a predefined set of identity formations. They do so *through knowledge* and *bodies* because they rely on pre-shared secrets (or asymmetric key knowledge) in the majority of cases or supposedly unique bodily presence in the minority.

In one way of thinking, the identity constructions that passwords allow are actually limited to a predefined set that is circular. The knowledge and bodies that passwords use as their proxy for an unformalized idea of personhood are supposed to verify that a specific subject *is* the bearer of the knowledge or the owner of the body, treating this as definition of personhood. In other words, this traditional way of thinking about passwords as *identity* means just that: a body that is presented for inspection is identical to a predefined body or knowledge spoken in response to a challenge is identical to pre-shared knowledge.

A second way of seeing this, however, ties the password to its function. In this paradigm, passwords do not identify people, but rather *use* knowledge and bodies to classify people into groups that serve a practical purpose. This is more akin to a system of classification such as 'allowed in' versus 'access denied'. Once more, though, this way of thinking is not well suited for displacing risk. Since, in this paradigm, passwords have nothing to do with an individual's *identity*, the burden of responsibility for misclassification is placed upon the classifier.

The broader philosophical stance of passwords as classification systems sits within various histories of thought and there are certainly many thinkers who have considered the logical relationship between an item and its taxonomy. Set theory, in mathematics, is one of the foremost examples of areas where this might be interesting. The other, though, is a formulation of classification that defies total encapsulation. For Theodor W. Adorno, for example, it is the case that 'objects do not go into their concepts without leaving a remainder'.[9] No process of classification is ever sufficient to capture human life. The *identity* that we might derive from a system of passwords is *not* identical to a person and cannot be so. In a very different context and as an unlikely co-holder of such a view, Jaron Lanier sees a similar phenomenon in the realm of social media, where the design decisions of software engineering tend to reduce our notion of people to pre-filled categories. For instance, Lanier asserts,

> The binary character at the core of software engineering tends to reappear at higher levels. It is far easier to tell a program to run or not to run, for instance, than it is to tell it to sort-of run. In the same way, it is easier to set up a rigid representation of human relationships on digital networks: on a typical social networking site, either you are designated to be in a couple or you are single (or you are in one of a few other predetermined states of being) – and that reduction of life is what gets broadcast between friends all the time.[10]

This problem is not, as Lanier states from his computational-centric worldview, unique to software. For centuries we have classified people using terms that are less than the sum of their whole. It is a quintessentially human thing to do.

The point is not then that passwords, particularly in the digital age, are somehow reductionist-classifying instruments. On their own, passwords do not contribute to the problems of classification outlined by Adorno and, in a different way, Lanier. It is, rather, that passwords require an interaction with such classifications to be of any use. Indeed, when I wrote that passwords 'produce identity', the missing question is: Identity with what? The answer cannot be discerned in a password itself as an abstraction, but only within the contexts of exclusion that these words of power enable. As it was at one point for the philosopher Ludwig Wittgenstein with language, so it is with passwords and society: 'The use of the word *in practice* is its meaning.'[11] Without thinking about what passwords do, what they are for and how we use them, we are able to say very little about their history and continued existence, their meaning.

•••• _

Passwords have appeared throughout human history in a variety of forms. While we most commonly conceive of passwords as instruments to verify who somebody is, it is my contention that they are in fact classification technologies that make no sense without an exclusionary context within which to operate. Passwords do not, in such thinking, verify somebody's identity. How could they? As I attempted to show in the preceding chapters on biometrics and identity, it is very hard to formalize a description of a person. People are not solely their bodies or their minds and, as humans, we intuitively recognize this. Machines or those without prior knowledge of an individual, however, cannot take that intuitive step for recognition and require a formal system's description language for human identity. To fulfil this need for formal descriptions, we can establish a series of proxy measures – passwords, biometrics, mathematical hashes – that can function as a loosely coupled approximation of a person's identity. However, passwords in all of their incarnations are never more than an approximation for identity. They represent an elision of the fact that we don't know how to describe a person fully and flawlessly to a machine or to someone with no prior knowledge of that individual.

We often forget this fact when we talk about passwords and the instances when they are compromised. This is how the rhetoric of identity theft can be possible and it is the reason why the argument that I am making here is more than a simple matter of semantics. When using the term 'identity theft', the password system has been considered to depict a total description of a person. It is this kind of thinking that can lead to absurd pronouncements, such as that in *Business Insider* recently where it was proclaimed that going through a 'major life event', such as getting married, put you at 'a higher risk of identity theft'. Feminist arguments about patriarchal cultures of marriage might agree with this, for different reasons. More seriously, though, it is on this basis that business consultants seek to shift the conversation to one of personal responsibility for the protection of identity (by which they mean passwords – a form of non-rivalrous knowledge), as though it were physical property. This manifests in claims that 'people need to take active ownership in protecting themselves' when, in fact, those verifying identity need to take better care in the design of their systems and responsibility for the weaknesses of the proxy measures that they choose.[12] In discourses of identity theft, passwords have become a full description of a person that, when stolen, dangerously change what you know into who you are.

At the same time, it is quite clear that passwords are inadequate measures for identifying people. The increasing frequency with which high-profile breaches are reported is a certain indicator of this fact. This aspect of passwords has, I contend, been known for many centuries and is most specifically seen in early literary representations. In ancient cultures of magic, such as the Assyrian and Egyptian rites of the dead, the words given to enter the underworld space were not actually concerned with identity at all; they were rather concerned with privilege. Those who could afford to have the words of entrance painted upon their funerary vessels would have the knowledge to cross into paradise. Not individual identification, then, but class distinction made on the grounds of worldly capital. For the Egyptians in particular here, the spells of class identification are meant to ensure an afterlife where only the materially virtuous (i.e. those who had inherited or come into wealth) would reach post-mortem safety.

Likewise, as covered above in my chapter on passwords in literature, tales such as *Ali Baba* are based around *defeating* passwords. The very fact that passwords cannot stand in for identity is what makes the narrative action of such a story possible. This is even present in the title of that tale; the 'forty thieves' are a class, a literary archetype of colluding malefactors and the password does not substitute for a single person. It is rather supposed to allow entrance for villains and deny access to protagonists, inverted over the course of the tale's narrative. *Ali Baba* can be read, in fact, as a warning of the disjunct between identity and its representation in passwords. The fact that the tale closes with Ali Baba as the *sole* possessor of the knowledge to enter the cave looks, superficially, as though order has been restored. Passwords are once more confined to individual identification. The preceding narrative, however, should warn us that the tale views identity and its proxies in a more complex light and that the narrative is, in this way, cyclical. The text seems to signal beyond its final page towards a day when Ali Baba will find himself usurped, made possible by his own overly strong faith in the technology of passwords.

The magic of the world of the *Harry Potter* books is also interesting in this respect. Unwilling to codify magic in such a way that anyone can perform it with a wand and the prerequisite knowledge, J. K. Rowling has, here, to fall back on a far older literary tradition: pure identification. It is not enough, in her fictional universe, to know and to have, the most common proxies that we use for granting or forbidding access. Instead, because her books deploy magic, she can insist that there is a predetermined class of people, wizards, who can do magic *simply because of who they are.* In Rowling's literary scenario, the measures that we usually want to stand in for identity (knowledge, bodies and possession of things), are mostly outshone by the notion that somebody just might be someone *for no reason* and *with no proxy.* It appears, superficially, as though you are either a wizard or you are not. Yet Rowling further complicates this idea through her presentation of 'squibs'; people of magical descent, in possession of a wand, with knowledge of spells but still unable to perform magic to any high standard. Rowling's use of 'squibs' signals her own knowledge that all of these proxies remain inadequate. Even genetic descent, in Rowling's world, is complicated as a measure of whether someone will be allowed access to the practice of magic.

This prodding at the foundation of identity is continued in various cinematic contexts. As I have shown from just a few examples, contemporary cinema has frequently undermined passwords as core narrative devices. In such varied contexts as *Demolition Man*, *Angels & Demons*, *Die Another Day*, *Alien: Resurrection*, *The Avengers* and *Minority Report* we see instances where supposedly infallible biometric password devices are subverted by the mutability (and mutilation) of the body. The way in which such films often present their degrading of passwords is through a body-mind split. In *Minority Report*, for example, as shown in a previous chapter, there is a link, but also a distinction, between the body and the mind. The protagonist wants access to the precognitive's mind but can only do so by stealing her body, thereby mirroring the master narrative of the film and repeating a cycle whereby individuals are praised only for their body, their mind or other characteristics, none of which can ever fully substitute for identity.

The other history that I charted was the fact that these problems of identity have often been most fully explored in military contexts. Those areas where there is potential for mass destruction have been among the pioneers in designing systems to verify who should be given this power. Persistent anxieties remain, however. Since the mathematicization of passwords in the 1970s through the development of one-way hashing algorithms, we have become increasingly reliant on technological mechanisms for which we do not possess full formal mathematical proof of soundness. As holes are eventually punched in the efficacy of existing algorithms, we depend upon the evolution of new methods at a pace that will outstrip the capacity of mathematicians to break them and of machines to brute-force crack them. It would take only one small breakthrough in contemporary mathematical theory to render our systems of secure communications and authentication (passwords) unusable. This would be catastrophic for the globalized practices of the World Wide Web that rely on remote identity verification. In the era of the atomic bomb, it could be even more devastating if linked to various command protocols for our weapons of annihilation.

It seems that, with the concomitant advancement in our technological capacity, we have expected passwords to become ever more flawless and congruent with some kind of pure identity for an individual. If anything, however, this is a dangerously naïve view. Should we discover ways of breaking the complex mathematical processes that currently underpin most of our passwords, the digital era of high personal and state security would rapidly unravel. Certainly, new biometric technologies will emerge but these will also come at a price, usually of personal privacy. The question that becomes interesting for 'identity theft' in that evolved world is whether, when somebody intercepts your genetic codes, they really are any closer to your identity than when they merely had knowledge.

Passwords may be inconvenient. They remain, however, the most commonly accepted way to determine the bounds of exclusion at a distance. Many of us interact with passwords multiple times per hour. As a ubiquitous technology, it is easy for us to think of passwords as a natural and obvious solution. In such a way, passwords as objects socially determine how we think, as I have attempted to demonstrate with the elisions inherent in the thinking around 'identity theft'. In another sense, though, passwords are only as useful as the needs that they serve. It is unlikely that the need to decide upon categories of inclusion/exclusion will vanish in the near future. How much closer we can get to a formalization of a person for the purposes of identity, either genetically or otherwise, remains to be seen. In the meantime, we will continue to entrust our finances, our national security and our privacy to the flawed, memorable phrases that we have developed over many centuries: passwords.

••••_

But what might the future of the password hold? Have we reached the final frontier for identifying and codifying individuals? Hardly. As we speak, smartphone manufacturers are working on an 'unlock' mechanism for their devices that will determine 'identity' through gait using motion sensors. It seems certain that as functional MRI techniques progress, unique brain-wave imaging/patterning will at some point enter the identification equation. Likewise, facial recognition marches on apace. Closer to the present, some outfits, such as Yahoo, are already replacing all passwords with one-time tokens, sent to a device that a user owns. Perhaps at some time we will see the introduction of immediate genetic sequencing that will allow extremely fast comparison of an individual's DNA to a copy held on file, a prospect that may terrify some privacy campaigners. At the same time, who can tell how quickly genetic engineering may advance and what measures people might take to modify their own genetic constitution in order to defeat such biometric systems of the future?

Can we conceive, though, of a day when 'Halt who goes there?' will not be understood? Certainly *Hamlet*'s speech pattern of 'unfold yourself' is no longer contemporary parlance, which is a shame, but we recognize the formulation of a password structure in the play so strongly that this is unproblematic. Might the time come, though, when an audience would not? Is it possible that our strongest means of tying identity to knowledge, property and the body could be deemed by the future to be so hopelessly naive and vulnerable that they would be a laughable concept? Alternatively, could notions of privacy be so radically transformed in a future society that there would be no need of structures like passwords because the inclusion/exclusion paradigm itself will have melted into air? There are both strains of utopian and dystopian thought that propose such futures, although a world without privacy probably most clearly summons George Orwell's *Nineteen Eighty-Four* [1949] to mind.

Continuing in this speculative vein, we might finally arrive at some of the stranger logical conclusions of thinking about passwords. If the ultimate system of passwords were one that had no proxies – a mode in which identity really did mean checking one person against another, *identical* individual – then the best password would be one in which people were cloned. In science/speculative fictional environments such as the world of *Star Trek*, such technology exists. The transporter devices in that fictional universe convert people into an 'energy pattern' that is then reconstructed into the same person at the target site. The energy pattern, in other words, must contain a perfect representation of the original human being for the re-materialization to work. In the film *The Prestige* [2006] this notion of duplication and teleportation is even more tightly coupled to identity as the plot twist (in which one of the cloned individuals must be killed each time) is mirrored in an identical twin scenario. In these fictions we see the seeds of perfect formalization of individuals that could lead to precise verification of identity, the most accomplished system of passwords possible. Is such a mode desirable? What are the ethical dilemmas behind such formalization? These questions and many more circle around the notions of subjectivity, identity and knowledge that are framed by passwords.

LIST OF ILLUSTRATIONS

NOTES

Introduction

1 Tung-Hui Hu, *A Prehistory of the Cloud* (Boston, MA: MIT Press, 2015), xviii.

2 A good number of these are also outlined in more detail in Peter Wisse, 'Semiotics of Identity Management,' in *The History of Information Security: A Comprehensive Handbook*, eds. Karl de Leeuw and Jan Bergstra (Amsterdam: Elsevier, 2007), 167–96.

3 When we turn to one-way hashing algorithms in Chapter 3, I will show that there is some upset of this timing dilemma.

4 M. Atif Qureshi, Arjumand Younus and Arslan Ahmed Khan, 'Philosophical Survey of Passwords,' *arXiv Preprint arXiv:0909.2367* (2009), 11, http://arxiv.org/abs/0909.2367.

5 Aeneas Tacitus, *Aineiou Poliorketika. Aeneas on Siegecraft*, trans. L. W. Hunter and S. A. Handford (Oxford: Clarendon Press, 1927), 61. Two-factor authentication, which will be covered below in more detail, is a form of identification that relies not only upon the respondent knowing the password, but also demonstrating that he or she possesses a specific object. A bank card is a good example of two-factor authentication: the user must know the Personal Identification Number (PIN) but he or she must also possess the card.

6   Robert McMillan, 'The World's First Computer Password? It Was Useless Too,' *WIRED*, 27 January 2012, http://www.wired.com/2012/01/computer-password/.

7   I am grateful to Jemima Matthews for a conversation on pass-spaces in April 2015.

Chapter 1

1   I owe this observation on disparities of scale to Joe Brooker.

2   Authentication usually refers to the process of verifying that someone is who they claim, while authorization is used to mean the process of checking that this same person is allowed to perform the action they have attempted.

3   Arthur Evans, *The Palace of Minos at Knossos: A Comparative Account of the Successive Stages of Early Cretan Civilization as Illustrated by the Discoveries at Knossos*, vol. 2 (London: Macmillan and Co., 1921), 60–92.

4   A. Shand, 'The Occupation of the Chatham Islands by the Maoris in 1835: Part II, The Migration of Ngatiawa to Chatham Island,' *The Journal of the Polynesian Society* 1, no. 3 (1892): 154–63.

5   Jonathan Haas, 'Warfare and the Evolution of Culture,' in *Archaeology at the Millennium: A Sourcebook*, ed. G. M. Feinman and T. D. Price (New York: Kluwer Academic/Plenum, 2001), 343.

6   Eva Horn, 'Logics of Political Secrecy,' *Theory, Culture & Society* 28, no. 7–8 (1 December 2011): 104, doi:10.1177/0263276411424583.

7 I draw heavily here on the work of the afore-cited Eva Horn.

8 All of the above from Horn, 'Logics of Political Secrecy,' 104–9.

9 Tacitus, *Aineiou Poliorketika. Aeneas on Siegecraft*, 61.

10 Ibid., 47, 63.

11 For more, see Jason Andress, 'Chapter 5 – Cryptography,' in *The Basics of Information Security*, 2nd edn (Boston: Syngress, 2014), 69–88, http://www.sciencedirect.com/science/article/pii/B9780128007440000051.

12 Recall that the 'second channel' refers to the need to pre-communicate a shared secret to a recipient in advance of sending the actual method.

13 Tacitus, *Aineiou Poliorketika. Aeneas on Siegecraft*, 75.

14 Ibid., 63.

15 Ibid., 77. Underlinings mine.

16 Think only of something like *The Hunt for Red October* [1990] to see this.

17 Tacitus, *Aineiou Poliorketika. Aeneas on Siegecraft*, 61.

18 Janet Abbate, *Inventing the Internet* (Cambridge, MA: The MIT Press, 2000), 144–5.

19 Ibid., 77.

20 Jennifer Wilcox, 'Solving the Enigma: History of the Cryptanalytic Bombe,' *Center for Cryptologic History, National Security Agency* (2006): 3, https://www.nsa.gov/about/_files/cryptologic_heritage/publications/wwii/solving_enigma.pdf. That's 3,000,000,000,000,000,000,000,000,000,000,000,000, 000,000,000,000,000,000,000,000,000,000,000,000,000,000 ,000,000,000,000,000,000,000,000,000 passwords. Much of this section is derived from Wilcox's excellent account.

21 I am thinking, here, primarily of *The Imitation Game* [2014] as a film that slightly overplays the contributions of individuals above team efforts, although it is true that Turing's efforts and intellect were remarkable.

22 Only three rotors were actually used at any time but it was impossible for cryptographers to establish which rotors were in use, thus substantially complicating the keyspace.

23 Technically, a probable-plaintext attack.

24 F. H. Hinsley, *Codebreakers: The Inside Story of Bletchley Park* (Oxford: Oxford University Press, 2001), 121.

25 Randall Monroe, 'Xkcd: Security,' *Xkcd*, 2009, https://xkcd.com/538/.

26 Clark Boyd, 'Profile: Gary McKinnon,' *BBC News*, 30 July 2008, sec. Technology, http://news.bbc.co.uk/1/hi/technology/4715612.stm.

27 Bruce Schneier, 'All or Nothing,' *CSO*, February 2007, 20.

Chapter 2

1 There are potentially Arabic origins for these tales, but they are not from the original *Nights*.

2 John Payne, *Alaeddin and the Enchanted Lamp* (London: Villon Society, 1889), chap. Introduction.

3 See Richard M. Stallman, 'Did You Say "Intellectual Property"? It's a Seductive Mirage,' *Gnu.org*, 20 April 2015, https://www.gnu.org/philosophy/not-ipr.en.html.

4 The Aarne-Thompson classification system of folklore traces similarities of plot structure in folk and fairy tales across many cultures then groups stories by these congruences.

5 The name of The Doctor has not so far been revealed to viewers of the television show (even though there have been various hints, explored thoroughly on fan websites if one wishes to search).

6 I here refer to the title of the first book by its original British name, whereas in the United States it was re-titled *Harry Potter and the Sorcerer's Stone*.

7 Passwords to Dumbledore's office include 'acid pops,' 'cockroach cluster,' 'fizzing whizbee,' 'lemon drop,' and 'sherbert lemon,' all types of confection. Passwords to the student common rooms include 'abstinence,' 'balderdash,' 'banana fritters,' 'baubles,' 'caput draconis,' 'dilligrout,' 'fairy lights,' 'flibbertigibbet,' 'fortuna major,' 'Mimbulus mimbletonia,' 'oddsbodikins,' 'pig snout,' 'pure-blood' (for the Slytherin common-room), 'quid agis,' 'scurvy cur,' 'tapeworm,' 'toffee éclairs' and 'wattlebird.' The password to the prefects' bathroom is 'pine fresh.'

8 Parselmouths mentioned in the series are: Herpo the Foul, Marvolo Gaunt, Morfin Gaunt, Harry Potter, Merope Riddle, Tom Marvolo Riddle (Lord Voldemort) and Salazar Slytherin.

9 J. K. Rowling, Open Book Tour, 19 October 2007, http://www.the-leaky-cauldron.org/2007/10/20/j-k-rowling-at-carnegie-hall-reveals-dumbledore-is-gay-neville-marries-hannah-abbott-and-scores-more.

10 While more advanced wizards in the world of *Harry Potter* can cast non-verbal spells, all students begin by learning incantations.

11 As I will go on to discuss, there are, of course, many complications to this such as the category of 'squib' that Rowling uses to denote someone of magical parentage but who has no wizarding aptitude.

12 Among the best of these is Walter J. Ong, *The Presence of the Word: Some Prolegomena for Cultural and Religious History* (New Haven, CT: Yale University Press, 1967).

13 I owe this last quip/observation to Christos Hadjioannou.

14 Scott B. Noegel, '"Sign, Sign, Everywhere a Sign": Script, Power, and Interpretation in the Ancient Near East,' in *Divination and Interpretation of Signs in the Ancient World*, ed. Amar Annus, Oriental Institute Seminars 6 (Chicago: Oriental Institute of the University of Chicago, 2010), 149.

15 Geraldine Pinch, *Magic in Ancient Egypt*, rev. edn (Austin: University of Texas Press, 2009), 69.

Chapter 3

1 See Alan Liu, *The Laws of Cool: Knowledge Work and the Culture of Information* (Chicago: University of Chicago Press, 2004), 76, for more of the ways in which these metaphors are confused.

2 There are many sources that can give more information on these metaphors of places. For a legal take, see Mark A. Lemley, 'Place and Cyberspace,' *California Law Review* 91, no. 2 (1 March 2003): 521–42, doi:10.2307/3481337.

3 Liu, *The Laws of Cool*, 42.

4 Those who seek a more mathematical and/or computer-science based approach would do well to consult either Bruce Schneier, *Applied Cryptography: Protocols, Algorithms and Source Code in C* (New York: John Wiley & Sons, 1995); or Alfred J. Menezes, Paul C. van Oorschot and Scott A. Vanstone, *Handbook of Applied Cryptography* (Boca Raton: CRC Press, 1996), from which much material in this chapter is distilled.

5   On the basis of being able to try 8,783,000 keys per second, a figure derived from http://calc.opensecurityresearch.com/.

6   While, for reasons of space, I won't deeply delve into the details of the mitigation against this, the defensive process is called 'salting' and it involves running the algorithm multiple times with a string appended to the end of the first round of hashing, thereby rendering this attack impotent.

7   Marc Stevens, 'Single-Block Collision Attack on MD5,' *IACR Cryptology ePrint Archive* (2012): 40, http://citeseerx.ist.psu.edu/viewdoc/download?doi=10.1.1.400.7023&rep=rep1&type=pdf ?.

8   Bart Preneel, 'The First 30 Years of Cryptographic Hash Functions and the NIST SHA-3 Competition,' in *Topics in Cryptology – CT-RSA 2010*, ed. Josef Pieprzyk, Lecture Notes in Computer Science 5985 (Berlin, Heidelberg: Springer, 2010): 30, http://link.springer.com/chapter/10.1007/978-3-642-11925-5_1.

9   On a strict time limit, he is forced at gunpoint to perform the hack while receiving oral sex from a prostitute.

10   There is a convention in descriptions of cryptography to use the character names 'Alice,' 'Bob' and 'Eve.'

11   A particularly pernicious version of this rhetoric can be seen in Robert David Steele, *The Open-Source Everything Manifesto: Transparency, Truth, and Trust* (Berkeley, CA: Evolver, 2012).

12   'Fake DigiNotar Web Certificate Risk to Iranians,' *BBC News*, 5 September 2011, http://www.bbc.co.uk/news/technology-14789763; Bruce Schneier, 'VeriSign Hacked, Successfully and Repeatedly, in 2010,' *Schneier on Security*, 3 February 2012, https://www.schneier.com/blog/archives/2012/02/verisign_hacked.html.

13   An aspect that is again interestingly explored in the Harry Potter series through legilimency and occlumency.

14 Russell Brandom, 'The Plot to Kill the Password,' *The Verge*, 15 April 2014, http://www.theverge.com/2014/4/15/5613704/the-plot-to-kill-the-password.

15 Anil K. Jain, Ruud Bolle and Sharath Pankanti, 'Introduction to Biometrics,' in *Biometrics: Personal Identification in Networked Society*, ed. Anil K. Jain, Ruud Bolle and Sharath Pankanti, The Kluwer International Series in Engineering and Computer Science, SECS 479 (Boston: Kluwer, 1999), 1–42.

16 'Borrowed Biometric Bypass,' *TV Tropes*, accessed 9 May 2015, http://tvtropes.org/pmwiki/pmwiki.php/Main/BorrowedBiometricBypass.

17 Yari Lanci, 'Remember Tomorrow: Biopolitics of Time in the Early Works of Philip K. Dick,' in *The World According to Philip K. Dick: Future Matters*, ed. Alexander Dunst and Stefan Schlensag (New York: Palgrave Macmillan, 2015), 111.

Chapter 4

1 United Kingdom, *Theft Act 1968*, accessed 23 May 2015, http://www.legislation.gov.uk/ukpga/1968/60/crossheading/definition-of-theft.

2 Jaron Lanier, *You Are Not a Gadget: A Manifesto* (London: Penguin Books, 2011), 102.

3 The Google Books corpus should be taken with a pinch of salt. The black box of its OCR mechanism and proprietary nature do not make it the best source for this type of mining. However, assuming that errors are standardized across the corpus, this nonetheless demonstrates an intriguing parallel rise in these terms.

4 United Kingdom, *Fraud Act 2006*, accessed 31 May 2015, http://www.legislation.gov.uk/ukpga/2006/35/contents.

5 For more on digital hygiene, see Hu, *A Prehistory of the Cloud*.

6 Confusingly, 'confessor' refers to the priest receiving the confession while the person confessing is the 'penitent'.

7 Foucault also links this form of truth telling back to earlier practices of parrhesia; plain speaking. See also Elizabeth Markovits, *The Politics of Sincerity: Plato, Frank Speech, and Democratic Judgment* (University Park, PA: Penn State University Press, 2008).

8 Umberto Eco, *The Role of the Reader: Explorations in the Semiotics of Texts* (Bloomington, IN: Indiana University Press, 1997), 85.

9 Theodor W. Adorno, *Negative Dialectics*, trans. E. B. Ashton (London: Routledge, 1973), 5.

10 Lanier, *You Are Not a Gadget*, 50.

11 Ludwig Wittgenstein, *Preliminary Studies for the 'Philosophical Investigations' (Blue and Brown Books)* (Oxford: Blackwell, 1972), 69.

12 Antonia Farzan, 'If You've Recently Done One of These 3 Things, You're at a Higher Risk for Having Your Identity Stolen,' *Business Insider*, 5 July 2015, http://www.businessinsider.com/highest-risk-of-identity-theft-2015-7.

INDEX

Page references for illustrations appear in *italics*.